SOLUTIONS
For the New Work Force

Solutions for the New Work Force

Policies for a New Social Contract

John J. Sweeney
and
Karen Nussbaum

Preface by Eli Ginzberg

Seven Locks Press
Cabin John, MD / Washington, DC

Copyright © 1989 Service Employees International Union
and 9to5, National Association of Working Women

Library of Congress Cataloging-in-Publication Data

Sweeney, John J., 1934-
  Solutions for the new work force.

  Bibliography: p.
  Includes index.
  1. Labor policy—United States. 2. Economic security—
United States. 3. Wages—United States. 4. Employee
fringe benefits—United States. 5. Service industries
workers—United States. 6. Work and family—United
States. I. Nussbaum, Karen. II. Title.
HD8072.5.S84   1989   331.1'0973   89-4252
ISBN 0-932020-62-3
ISBN 0-932020-63-1 (pbk.)

Manufactured in the United States of America
Cover Design by Marty Anderson Design
Typesetting by Letterforms Typography
Printed by Aracata Graphics Co., Kingsport, TN

Printed on acid-free paper.

For more information write or call:

Seven Locks Press
P.O. Box 27
Cabin John, MD 20818
(301) 320-2130

To the women and men
whose daily struggle to build
a better tomorrow
is building
a better future for us all:
Members of
the Service Employees International Union
and 9to5, National Association of Working Women.

Contents

Preface

When John Sweeney invited me to write the *foreword* to a book that was still in preparation, I said yes without waiting to review the analysis and the proposed solutions. I felt confident, based on the Service Employees/9to5 Conference in which I had participated in September 1987, that such a book would contribute constructively toward a deepening public understanding of the new work force and would help point the way to improved public policies.

I am pleased to report that my confidence has proved to be fully justified. Of course, this does not mean that I or any other informed reader will necessarily agree with all the arguments and conclusions. But no sensible person would expect a policy tract to command 100 percent approval.

Let me emphasize the major strengths of the present work:

—It identifies clearly, with revealing charts and graphs, the serious weaknesses that have developed among many groups in the working population between the early 1970s and today.

—It argues persuasively that business leadership's simplistic approach to turning around the U.S. economy—by cutting wages and fringe benefits to realize increased productivity and more rapid growth—is a no-win approach despite the fact that it has dominated the Reagan era.

—It calls attention to a number of critical policy issues dealing with health insurance, private pensions, child care, safety in the work place, and investment in training and retraining, where benefits have been eroded, coverage has been reduced, or private and public policy have not as yet even reached the point of taking the first constructive steps toward remedying serious shortcomings.

The U.S. economy, despite claims of the Reagan enthusiasts, is in serious trouble, and as *Solutions for the New Work Force* makes clear, the economy cannot be turned around further by eroding the wages and working conditions of those in the lower half of the income distribution. We must do just the opposite and pursue an investment strategy aimed at improving the competencies and skills of all members of the work force, present and prospective, and at ensuring that everybody able and willing to work has an opportunity to do so. Turning our economy around requires that everybody has a role to play, including members of the underclass, people living in poverty, the large number of unemployed. A progressive U.S. economy cannot afford to tolerate or condone their exclusion.

Eli Ginzberg, Director
Conservation of Human Resources
Columbia University

Acknowledgments

The success of any project is the result of a collective effort, and this book is no exception.

The genesis of this book was a conference entitled "Solutions for the New Workforce" jointly sponsored by the Service Employees Union (AFL-CIO, CLC) and 9to5, National Association of Working Women in September 1987. The enthusiasm, excitement and thirst for new approaches to problems confronting the American workers provided the impetus to us to collect our thoughts and theirs and to share this knowledge with a broad audience. We thank the participants for their vital contribution to this book. Our special thanks go to those who have allowed us to use their experiences and observations on particular issues to help make this book more relevant to our readers.

The encouragement and support of the leadership of SEIU and 9to5 over the last year was essential to the completion of the project. We thank SEIU Secretary-Treasurer Richard W. Cordtz, members of the SEIU Executive Board, the 9to5 Board, and the Working Women's Education Fund for their continued commitment to a policy agenda that addresses the needs of all working people.

We want to thank Bob Welsh and the members of the SEIU and 9to5 staff who worked so hard to turn this book from a concept into a reality. They have brought intelligence, dedication, and good humor to this project.

Without the assistance of Ellen Cassedy, Peggy Connerton, Debbie Goldman, and Cathy Schoen, the book would not have been written. Cathy, in particular, framed the analysis throughout the book; Debbie researched much of the material in chapters 3, 5, 6 and 7; Peggy lent her expertise on chapters 4, 5, 6, and 7; and Ellen made sure we said it all coherently and elegantly. Jean Ross contributed thoughtful comments on endless drafts. Marcia McGill coordinated the effort and saw the process through, from start to finish.

In addition, JoAnne Browne, Bill Borwegen, Sharon Dannan, Meg Lewis, Liz McNichol, Carol Regan, Gerry Shea, Kathy

Skrabut, and Carolyn York provided useful comments on individual chapters. Vicki O'Reilly, Rob Vitello, Susan Cole, and Sheri Roberts provided technical assistance and research. Pat Kennedy and Christine Taylor provided typing assistance on numerous drafts.

We also want to thank our publisher and editor at Seven Locks Press, James McGrath Morris and Jane Gold, who improved the final product with their intelligent criticisms and suggestions.

As a new Administration looks to develop policies to lead us into the decade of the 1990s, we think the message of this book is more important than ever; that the only way to strengthen the U.S. economy is to invest in our most valuable resource—our people. This book describes practical proposals that move us closer to the fulfillment of the American dream for all working men and women.

Introduction

Newspaper headlines, sophisticated research reports, and daily personal experience are all reaching the same conclusion in the 1980s: these are troubling times for Americans who must work for a living.

Who are these Americans? They are people like the clerical worker in Milwaukee who had a heart attack and bypass surgery. She has three part-time jobs but no health insurance—none of her jobs provided benefits.

Like the baker on the night shift at Mr. Donut in Philadelphia, who was fired from his $17,000-a-year job when he took three days off to take his infant Down's syndrome daughter to the hospital for emergency surgery. Now his wife supports him and their two adopted, disabled children on a secretary's salary.

Or like the former automobile worker who moved his family to Los Angeles from Detroit in search of work. Both he and his wife found work but their combined minimum-wage income fails to pay the rent. The family is now one of LA's homeless.

These people are part of a new work force, characterized by marginal working conditions, shaped by the influx of women, and struggling under policies that have shifted the responsibility for health and welfare off employers and government squarely onto the shoulders of the overburdened working family. For them, change too often has become the enemy, bringing pay, benefit, and job loss rather than improved living standards.

This book grows out of the experience of members of this new work force, led by the women and men working in the booming service sector of the economy. We know these people well; as president of the Service Employees Union (SEIU), one of the largest service sector unions, and executive director of 9to5, the nation's leading organization for working women, we work with them daily. Their lives and working conditions are set by management's response to the new economic realities.

Despite the past six years—the longest peacetime "expansion" since World War II—average family income has barely returned to levels achieved 15 years ago. And more low- and middle-income families fail to reach the average; income inequality is sharply up. Moreover cuts in job based health insurance and pension coverage have pushed family living standards still lower. As a result, although more people per family are working for wages due to women's dramatic entry into the paid work force, most families are losing ground.

Life is less secure. Business policies, coupled with intensified international competition and technological change, are creating and destroying jobs at an accelerating pace. Restructuring through automation and business mergers has disrupted individual careers and entire communities overnight. *Fortune* magazine estimates that 40 million people have suffered wrenching change in the 1980s alone. Forecasts predict the pace will quicken: given current trends people should expect to change not just jobs but careers three or four times in their lifetimes. Yet no social or job-based policies exist to help people learn new skills or make the transition to new jobs.

At the national level, massive federal and international deficits paralyze and threaten to eliminate traditional social policy levers that could otherwise channel business activity toward the good of the nation. Advocates of the status quo claim, whatever the evidence of decline in living standards, that more sacrifice from middle and low income families is necessary for the U.S. to compete successfully in an emerging global economy.

This book argues that we have a choice. We are in the midst of dramatic structural change in the domestic and world economy but the challenge before us is to turn change into progress rather than despair for the work force and family. Our central argument is twofold: First, current corporate workplace policies and the nation's failure to develop new social policies threaten the work force and the future of the United States in a more competitive world economy. Second, there *are* solutions—new policies geared to meet the needs of a new work force and new economic realities.

Around the world other countries provide us with models. At home, cities, states and a few joint employer-union agreements are pioneering new programs and policies. A national conference in September 1987, cosponsored by the Service Employees Union and 9to5, National Association of Working Women, brought policy makers and activists together to share the models and develop "Solutions for the New Workforce".

This book draws from strategies presented at the conference. Each chapter documents the need for new work and family policies and outlines policy options that address specific problems.

Chapter 1 documents basic income, inequality, and poverty trends and the shift in job policies that have transformed the historic march toward a service economy and job growth from a story of prosperity to one of decline. A binge of mergers and takeovers has wasted workers' sacrifices, absorbing short-term profits in paper exchanges rather than productive activity. Growth in productivity has slowed as insecurity and increased inequality have proven poor motivators to work or innovate. As a result, other industrial countries are now taking the lead.

The following three chapters document a pervasive employer strategy to create a more disposable work force with fewer ties or claims on business.

Chapter 2 reviews the loss of higher-wage jobs and outlines an attack on wage standards as evidence of the need for new efforts to raise wage and equity standards.

Chapter 3 focuses on an emerging "contingent" or "marginal" work force in which more than one out of every four jobs is part time, temporary or contracted rather than full-time. And it discusses the need for new policies to curb exploitation while providing people with job flexibility.

Chapter 4 documents the rapid reduction in health and pension benefits for working families, discusses the structural changes behind the trends, and presents case histories of a growing movement to require basic benefits for all.

Next, chapter 5 analyzes the growing conflict between work and family. Today the vast majority of women expect and are expected to work for wages. This revolutionary and permanent shift in family life has rapidly expanded the supply of a skilled and educated work force to the benefit of business and the nation. Corporations, however, have largely exploited women's labor with substandard jobs and have failed to address the heightened conflicts between work and the needs of the family, especially the care and nurturing of children and older relatives. These conflicts, if left unresolved, further threaten the quality of life for generations to come and undermine efforts to improve productivity. The United States now lags far behind virtually all industrialized countries in responding. The chapter concludes with an agenda for community- and job-based child care and family leave policies.

Aiming for lower rather than the highest living standards, U.S. job policies have also failed to provide training and retraining necessary to help workers of all ages keep pace with a changing world order. With no job security, people fear and resist rather than work for change.

Chapter 6 argues that we will all lose as Japan, West Germany, France, Sweden and other industrialized countries compete with us by mastering information-age technology with a skilled work force capable of rapid responses and an ability to adapt and innovate. It concludes with an education and training agenda for helping people adjust to, master, and control change.

The shift of jobs toward service industries and away from manufacturing holds out the promise of cleaner, safer work in which people have more control of their work life than they do on the assembly line. But service industry jobs and new technology have brought with them new hazards and new forms of sweatshop, high-stress working conditions.

Chapter 7 surveys health, safety and working conditions in the workplace and describes policy efforts to improve dignity and control of work as well as to reduce job hazards.

A desire for changes is building across the country. Public opinion polls repeatedly show that broad political support exists for making investment in people the central goal of the economy.

Chapter 8 outlines a set of investment, tax and spending practices to build economic strength and ensure future economic growth.

Almost 60 years ago, short-sighted policies brought the world economy to a shattering halt. The result was the Great Depression. What business thought was good for business—a narrow focus on short-term profits and the bottom line—was clearly good for neither business nor working families.

Out of the despair and conflict of the depression grew a new social contract that made the employment and the well-being of the work force a central goal of public and corporate policies. The minimum wage, child labor laws, the 40-hour week, Social Security, and the rights of workers to organize into unions all were part of a developing agreement to harness living standards of families to corporate growth by broadening the claims of the work force on the conditions of their labor.

As men and women fall to lower income standards, the pressure for change and new social policies mounts. New state and local government legislation has begun to formulate a set of ground rules for the women and men who must work for a living. The long-term policy goal is to put job standards and equity back at center stage in national and local economic policy. It's time to put the economy back to work for working families—for ourselves and our children.

The stakes are too high for any of us to sit on the sidelines.

SOLUTIONS
For the New Work Force

[In the increasingly competitive world economy since the 1970s,], big business had essentially four options. They could, of course, go back to basics, offering the consumer new or improved products. They could get out of the producing end altogether and find alternative ways to make paper profits. They could, in the words of President Nixon's Assistant Secretary of Labor, Arnold Weber, "zap labor." Or they could make a new bid to control government so as to reduce their taxes and their regulatory costs. In fact, we now know that big business chose the last three.

—Bennett Harrison, professor
of political economy and planning,
Massachusetts Institute of Technology,
in an address to the Conference on Solutions
for the New Workforce, Washington, D.C.,

What kind of economic choices can we make to make sure we have room for everybody in the society to participate in the world of work? If you have any respect and concern about the survival of your society, you had better make sure that everybody has a place in it.

—Eli Ginzberg, director of
conservation of human resources,
Hepburn Professor Emeritus of Economics
at the Graduate School of Business,
Columbia University.

Every American generation has left the next with a better living standard. Unless we change course, we will be the first to fail to do so.

—Ira Magaziner, president of Telesis,
an international consulting firm.

Chapter 1:
Hardships for Working Families: A Corporate Choice

The Way It Was: Jobs Meant Prosperity

Until the 1970s, most families in the United States could answer "yes" to the question, "Are you better off than your parents?" And until the 1970s, parents could expect an even better life for their children. For 25 years following World War II, the U.S. economy produced an expanding middle class, a steady rise in the standard of living, and a consistent improvement in working conditions. Average family income adjusted for inflation doubled by 1973. Inequality of income and wealth narrowed. Poverty dropped to a historic low, from 17 percent in the 1960s down to 11 percent in the 1970s.[1] By and large, those who were willing and able to work had the opportunity to share in the American dream.

At the outset of the 1970s, economists and politicians were proclaiming the dawn of a new "postindustrial era." Farms and factories, having long since ceased to be the major source of jobs, gave way to offices, hospitals, banks, and stores.[2] The advent of the computer age created new possibilities for turning over monotonous or dangerous work to machines, freeing people for creative careers at clean, safe work sites. New technology also offered the potential for increased leisure time and greater equality: people could

5

produce more with less effort, and more workers could be trained to carry out jobs requiring thought, judgment, and social skills. A service economy appeared to offer hope for a still better tomorrow.

Moreover, the civil rights movement had won new promises for job opportunity and equity at work. The women's movement followed on its heels, and women entered the paid work force in record numbers, changing family work patterns and demanding equality. Minorities and women were now the majority of the new work force.

A social contract between business and labor dating back to the bitter battles and despair of the 1930s ensured the sharing of prosperity. Unlike Europe, where laws set standards for health coverage, job training, layoffs, and leave policies, the United States did not rely heavily on government action to make this promise a reality. Public policies *did* guarantee a minimum wage and a retirement income floor (Social Security), outlawed discrimination, set health and safety standards, and granted workers limited rights to collective action. Beyond these minimal standards, however, job policies were largely a matter of negotiation between employers and unions or individual workers, negotiation that depended on an implicit agreement with business that the well-being of the work force would be a central corporate goal. And for the most part, major corporations kept their side of the bargain. Key unionized manufacturing industries set job standards for the entire economy. A union job meant security, the opportunity for advancement, and the ability to support a family.

Job growth itself was a signal of prosperity. More jobs meant more families working. Work meant a chance for a decent standard of living. An increase in the number of workers meant rising family income. Wages and benefits improved across industries. Federal policy adjusted the minimum wage so that it equaled at least half the average hourly wage. In all, the ground rules appeared to be working. Change brought progress and a rising standard of living.

1970s and 1980s:
Stagnation and Decline, and Inequality

But the 1970s turned out to be the end of an era, not a new beginning. Despite an illusion of economic growth, by 1988 average family income[3] barely matched the levels achieved in the early 1970s (the standard of living for low- and middle-income working families had peaked in 1973), and it has taken 6 years of peacetime expansion—the longest such period in postwar history—to climb back up to the level achieved 15 years ago.[4] And this is so even though more people are working and more families than ever before are relying on income from two or three jobs.

The stagnation in income hides an even more alarming trend: a growing inequality in income distribution in our country. Family income has fallen precipitously for low- and middle-income families. As of 1985, the bottom 20 percent of families were struggling to live on one-third less than they did in the early 1970s (figure 1.1, next page). Fewer and fewer families today are achieving yesterday's middle incomes.[5]

Further, of those families at the very bottom of the economic scale, an increasing number are unable to work their way out of poverty. By the end of 1987, 32.4 million lived in poverty, nearly 10 million more than in 1973.

Today's poverty mainly strikes those under age 65. Thanks to Social Security support programs, poverty rates for senior citizens have declined; however, over one-fifth of all children now live in poverty (figure 1.2 on following page) even though their parents are more likely to be employed than they were in the past. Of the 14.4 million poor adults who were able to work, almost two-thirds did, yet their jobs didn't pay enough to pull the family out of poverty.[6] And only the remnants of the 1960s War on Poverty programs have stemmed a still greater increase in poverty. According to the Urban Institute, without social support for food, housing, health, and income, an additional 5 to 12 million would be poor.[7]

Figure 1.1: Average Annual Income for Families with Children, 1973 and 1985

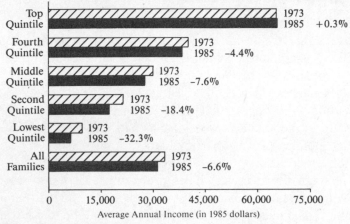

Average Annual Income (in 1985 dollars)

Source: Sheldon Danziger and Peter Gottschalk. "Target Support at Children and Families," *New York Times, 22 March, 1987, sec. 3, p. 2.*

Figure 1.2: Increase in Poverty by Family Type, 1960-87

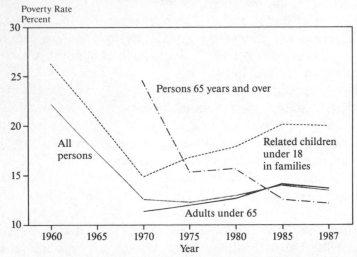

Note: No 1960 or 1965 data exists for those 65 and over or for adults under 65.

Source: Bureau of the Census, *Money Income and Poverty Status in the United States,* 1987, Table 18.

Yet, the rich have done well in stark contrast to the stagnation and decline of families at the bottom. The heads of corporations and the top owners of the nation's wealth pull in 30 percent more than they did in 1973. These top 5 percent of families now claim a greater share of national income than the bottom 40 percent.[9]

And, the richest families now claim a greater share of wealth than they did in 1973. In a 1983 study of wealth, the Federal Reserve Board found that the richest 10 percent held 92 percent of municipal bonds, 85 percent of all stocks, and 64 percent—nearly two-thirds—of all financial assets. Moreover, the super rich, the top one-half of 1 percent, owned nearly 50 percent of all non-residential wealth, and this segment has succeeded in increasing its share of wealth by over one-third since the 1970s.[10] Put simply, today's richest 3 million families have more to live on than do the nation's 26 million low- and lower-middle income families put together.

Figure 1.3: Property vs. Labor Income, 1970-87

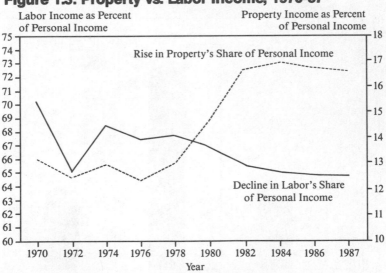

Note: Labor income consists of wages, salaries and other labor income.

Source: *Economic Report of the President,* 1988, table B-25.

Pay and wealth are up because ownership of wealth brought in high levels of income. In fact, between 1970 and 1987, the boom in property income (interest, dividends, and rents) so overshadowed wage income that labor's share of total personal income plummeted (figure 1.3, previous page). Employment earnings now make up only 65 percent of average personal income, compared with 70 percent in 1970. And in the meantime, the middle class is shrinking. Today more families fall into the low and high ends of the income distribution while fewer families enjoy an 'average'' or "middle" income. This can be illustrated most simply by dividing all families into high-, middle-, and low- income classes with fixed income divisions between groups. After adjustment for inflation, the number of families earning between $15,000 and $50,000 declined from 1973 to 1987 while the number of families at the bottom and top went up (figure 1.4).

Figure 1.4:
Changes in Family Income Distribution, 1973 and 1987

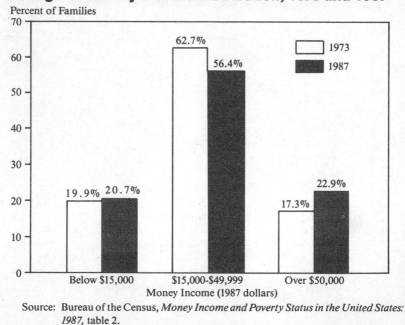

Percent of Families

Money Income (1987 dollars)

Source: Bureau of the Census, *Money Income and Poverty Status in the United States: 1987,* table 2.

Thus, with income declining for many families and increasing for a smaller number at the top, America is clearly in the midst of a major redistribution of income, one that is more unequal now, at the end of the 1980s, than it has been at any time in postwar history. Moreover, inequality is rising across the nation. And increased inequality, coming on top of slow growth in national income during the 1980s, has heightened a sense of decline and unfairness.

People Are Working Harder but Losing Ground

Families are doing their best to save their standard of living by working harder (table 1.1). Among working-age adults, 71 percent hold jobs—an all-time high.[11] More people are working two or more jobs than ever before. More families are sending two or more people out to work. Even most mothers with infants are working.

Table 1.1: Participation in the Work Force, by Selected Groups, 1975-87

	1975	1980	1987
Labor Force Participation, population under 65[a]	63.1%	67.2%	70.7%
Workers with two or more jobs in thousands[b]	4.6%	4.9%	5.4%
Families with children with two or more wage earners[c]	52.4%	59.6%	66.8%
Working Mothers with infants under age[d]	31.5%	39.2%	51.9%

[a]Bureau of Labor Statistics (BLS), *Handbook of Labor Statistics* (June 1985), tables 3 and 15; BLS, *Employment and Earnings* (January 1988), table 3.

[b]J. F. Stinson, Jr., "Moonlighting by Women Jumped to Record Highs," *Monthly Labor Review* (November 1986), table 1.

[c]Data start in 1977. BLS, "News Release USDL 87-345," 12 August 1987, table 4; BLS, "News Release USDL 86- 345," 20 August 1986, table 4.

[d]BLS, "News Release USDL 87-345," 12 August 1987, table 1; additional BLS data.

An explosion in job growth—a net increase of 20 million jobs in the past 10 years—has made this increased work effort possible. There was a time when this explosion in job growth and work effort would have been cause for celebration. But not any longer. Only the revolutionary increase in women working for wages has saved family incomes from a steep decline. Congress's Joint Economic Committee estimates that family income would have plummeted 18 percent in the 1980s had women not gone to work.[12] Moonlighting (working at night) and holding extra jobs have also helped families stay even. By 1987, 5.7 million people were supplementing their income in this way—a 20.4 percent jump since 1980.[13] In effect, a family today must work an average of one day more per week just to hold on to the income levels of the early 1970s (figure 1.5).

Figure 1.5: Job Growth
and Declining Family Income, 1970-87

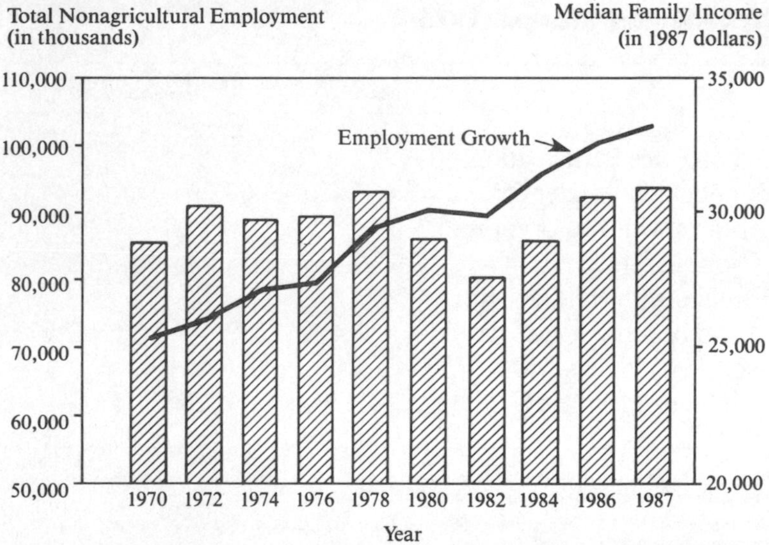

Total Nonagricultural Employment
(in thousands)

Median Family Income
(in 1987 dollars)

Sources: Bureau of Labor Statistics, *Employment and Earnings* (March 1988), table B-1;
Bureau of the Census, *Money Income and Poverty Status in the United States:*
1987, table A.

And despite all this effort, for the first time since the Great Depression, most workers can expect to earn less than their parents. In the 1950s and 1960s, young men could expect that by age 30, they would be making a third more than their fathers had as young men.[14] But by 1983, 30-year-old men were making 10 percent less than their fathers had. Similarly, today's young workers are earning 20 to 25 percent less (adjusted for inflation) than their counterparts 10 years ago; young women earn less than young women did then, and a chronic male-female wage gap persists.[15]

Family income is down for one simple reason: wages are down. For most families, earnings from work are nearly the sole source of income; only the wealthy derive considerable income from other sources. Across all families, 73 percent of all income, on average, comes from work.[16] But, as illustrated by figure 1.6, average hourly wages are down 7 percent and weekly wages are down 15 percent since 1973, despite some recovery in the 1980s.

Figure 1.6: Hourly and Weekly Wage Trend, 1960-87

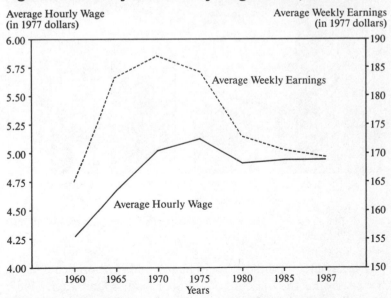

Source: Economic Report of the President, 1988, tables B-44 and B-45.

Although an increasingly skilled work force and a more complex economy could be expected to result in a more equal distribution of wages, with jobs at the bottom moving up, more than half of all people today earn less than $12,500 per year—counting earnings of part-time workers. For the 44 percent of the people working full-time, year-round, half earn less than $22,380, and earnings are now concentrated at the bottom and the top for both women and men (figure 1.7).[17]

Figure 1.7: Median Income, by Sex (Persons 14 and Over), 1987

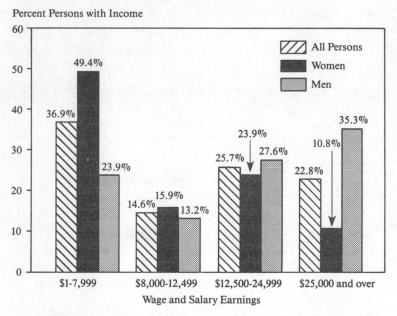

Percent Persons with Income

Source: Bureau of the Census, *Money Income and Poverty Status in the United States: 1987,* table 12.

The decline of employer-paid health and pension benefits has further eroded the standard of living of today's families. By 1987, 37 million people had no health insurance—three out of four of them were workers or their dependents. Less than half of all workers today are covered by pension plans, and the proportion is declining.[18]

Clearly, the expectations that more jobs and harder work would increase living standards have not been met. Even six years of sustained economic growth have not eased the pressures on working families who are trying to achieve or maintain middle- class standards of living. And the trends starkly depart from the rest of recent history when jobs, indeed, meant prosperity.

To explain all these problems—poverty, rising inequality, stagnant or declining income—some would cite both the rapid growth of service industry jobs, which have accounted for virtually all job growth over the past decade, and more intense international competition. A closer look at our economy, however, reveals this not to be the case.

The United States as a Service Economy

The term *service economy* may bring to mind a picture of corner stores and laundromats—small businesses that operate on a local scale and generate only small profits. How could a "mom and pop" store possibly bring us as much prosperity as a steel mill? Thus, the dominant economic role of service industries takes the blame for inequality and slow growth.

Historically, however, the evolution of a service economy—one in which most jobs are neither on farms nor in factories but in an array of service industries—has signaled prosperity, not only in the United States but in country after country around the world. The transformation of the U.S. economy to one based on services has been ongoing since World War II, when the growing complexity of our economy began to require an advanced network of communication, transportation, and financial services. For the first 25 years, that transformation brought a doubling of income standards. And rising income plus more leisure time meant people could enjoy more personal and community services. Clearly, then, service jobs do not inherently lead to lower living standards.

Nor do they eliminate other jobs. Service industries have not sup-
planted the manufacturing sector; instead, services have developed
to support manufacturing in a more complex world. Most service
workers (60 percent) package, finance, insure, distribute, or sell
manufactured goods. And many jobs that were once performed
in-house and called manufacturing jobs are now counted in the
"service industry" category as services performed on contract for
industrial firms. The employer has shifted but not the work.[19]

As for where the service jobs are in our economy, consider the
following:

—Hospitals employ twice as many people as auto and steel
combined.

—In business services job increases alone equalled the total
number of people producing electrical and electronic equipment from 1978 to 1986.

—Jobs in retail food stores exceed total agricultural employment.

—Clerical workers outnumber manufacturing workers.

—Janitorial, clerical, sales and health and food service jobs
account for 7 out of the 10 occupations with the largest projected job growth.

The image of Main Street versus Wall Street—of "mom and
pop" stores versus corporations—also couldn't be further from the
truth. The U.S. service sector is big business, and its corporate giants
are often indistinguishable from their industrial brothers. *Fortune*
magazine now tracks both a Service 500 and an Industrial 500. In
recent years, many corporations have alternated between the two
lists as empires split off and repurchased new lines of business. For
example, American Can once made cans; now it is called Primerica
and it produces financial services. Greyhound at one time operated
buses; now it also provides food processing and other services.

Although most people in today's economy work at sites with
fewer than 100 people[20] their employers tend to be large corporations. Nearly one in four workers are employed directly by one of

these giant corporations. Millions more work for them indirectly in contracted, temporary, and consultant positions.

With the development of the service economy, then, the dominant role of giant corporations has increased, not diminished. For example, as of 1988:

—**ARA HOLDING** (food and other contract services) sales now nearly equal those of the **Deere Equipment Company**— 14 billion compared with $4.1 billion.

—**McDonald's** sales now exceed those of **Bethlehem Steel**—$4.9 billion compared with $4.6 billion.

—**Prudential of America**'s net gain of $930 million tops all major drug companies and rivals leading oil companies.

—Five health care corporations each top $2 billion in revenues.

—**Kelly** (clerical) and **Servicemaster** (cleaning) temporary and contract services each earn more than $1 billion, exceeding the revenues of *more than 200* of the top Fortune 500 Industrials.

—**Beverly Enterprises** (a nursing home chain) employs more people than **Dow Chemical** and **Monsanto** combined—110,000 at Beverly compared with 53,000 and 50,000, respectively, at the two chemical companies.

—**Sears Roebuck** employs more people (500,000) than any industrial corporation except **General Motors** (813,400) and as many people as the combined work force of the top 34 U.S. industrial and farm equipment companies (525,000), and dwarfs IBM (389,000).

Moreover, as illustrated in table 1.2 (see next page), the combined sales of the largest corporations account for most of the total national product, and the combined after-tax profits of this group were equal to the total net profits for all businesses combined since profits and losses of all smaller companies offset one another.

Table 1.2: Giant Service and Industrial Corporations' Domination of U.S. Economy

	1987 Total	% of Economy
Service 500		
Employment	10.3 million	10.1 %
Sales	$1,226.7 billion	27 %
Profits		
(net after tax)	$47.6 billion	34 %
Industrial 500		
Employment	3.1 million	12.8 %
Sales	$1,879.5 billion	41.9 %
Profits		
(net after tax)	$90.6 billion	65.8 %

Notes: BLS, *Employment and Earnings*, March, 1988.
Sources: "The Service 500," *Fortune*, 6 June 1988; "The Industrial 500," *Fortune*, 25 April 1988.

The only thing that is small about the service economy tends to be the paychecks. Of the ten jobs projected to grow most quickly over the next decade, 8 pay less than median income ($19,396) and 5 pay poverty wages—less than $12,000 per year on average (figure 1.8)

Pay remains at the bottom even for employees of the Service 500, with their giant assets. Some members of the Service 500 make taxpayers subsidize their workers rather than provide decent wages and benefits. Nursing home employees of Beverly Enterprises (a $2 billion corporation), for example, qualify for medical assistance and food stamps.[21] And whereas, in the past, service job standards played catch-up with those in the manufacturing sector, today the tables are turned. Although service positions often require more skills and training, service employers take the lead in setting trends for lower and more unequal job standards, and manufacturing standards are coming down to match the low pay of service employers.[22]

Thus, it is not the *nature* of service jobs that accounts for the growing hardships for working families. Rather, the culprit is a dramatic, systematic shift in corporate job policy. The deliberate choices of service industry leaders are responsible for the stagnation, decline, and inequality, and things could get worse. A recent study warned that, given the current choice of technology trends and job standards, further development toward service industries could decrease the "middle" group of occupations by one-third by the end of the 1990s.[23]

Figure 1.8: Fastest Growing Jobs (Projected), 1986-2000

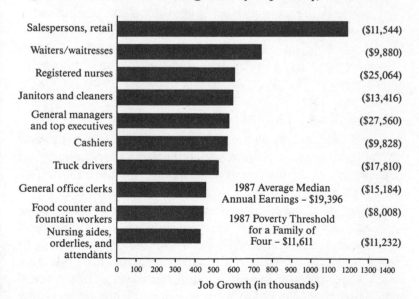

Salespersons, retail	($11,544)
Waiters/waitresses	($9,880)
Registered nurses	($25,064)
Janitors and cleaners	($13,416)
General managers and top executives	($27,560)
Cashiers	($9,828)
Truck drivers	($17,810)
General office clerks	($15,184)
Food counter and fountain workers	($8,008)
Nursing aides, orderlies, and attendants	($11,232)

1987 Average Median Annual Earnings – $19,396

1987 Poverty Threshold for a Family of Four – $11,611

Job Growth (in thousands)

Sources: G.T. Silvestri and J.M. Lukasiewicz, "A Look at Occupational Employment Trends to the Year 2000," *Monthly Labor Review* (September 1987), table 5; Bureau of Labor Statistics, unpublished data.

Corporate America and International Competition

For their part, corporations blame international competition for forcing business to impose inequality and lower wages on the work force. Reducing labor costs, the argument goes, frees up funds for investment and keeps prices down so that American products can compete with those from low-wage nations. Corporate leaders suggest further that working families may need to sacrifice to fund the technological innovations necessary if the United States is to keep pace with its competitors. In fact, however, international competition has presented corporate America not with a mandate but, instead, with a set of choices.

During the 1950s and 1960s, corporations could easily afford to share their wealth for at that time the United States dominated the world economy with few challenges. As *Business Week* observed,

> Churning out profits in an era of keen global competition and low worldwide inflation is a new experience for American CEOs.... [P]ost war CEOs usually neglect to tell you that they not only had a level playing field, they had an empty one. The famous Harvard business school class of 1949 didn't do too well once the Japanese showed up, to say nothing of raiders like Carl Icahn or Irwin Jacobs.[24]

The growth and rebuilding of the rest of the industrialized world in the 1970s caught U.S. managers and policymakers sleeping and challenged U.S. domination of world markets for the first time. Past failure to innovate and invest left key American industries deeply vulnerable to rising energy prices and the new competition from abroad.[25] U.S. dominance of mass production was the most vulnerable of all. By the 1970s, Third World countries had developed mass production capacity and could, for the first time, compete. With wages and working conditions far below those of the industrialized world, Third World production threatened to render obsolete mass manufacturing in the United States. Moreover, European and Japanese multinational corporations now vied with U.S.

multi-national corporate giants as new transportation and communication networks enabled them to flourish by moving production and distribution sites rapidly around the world.

In this new economic environment, U.S. corporate managers wanting to produce at home had two basic choices: 1) to improve product quality and boost productivity through investment, training, and innovation; or 2) to make U.S. products cheaper by lowering job standards for working families. The first choice would require using existing funds for investment and asking stockholders and top management to wait for longer-term gains. It also would require using innovation and advanced technology to develop the full potential of a skilled, educated labor force. The second choice would be to hang on to short-term profits by requiring sacrifices from working people.

With the entry of women into the wage work force coincident with the coming of age of the baby boom generation, corporations had the advantage of an expanding labor supply. Lowering labor costs offered an apparently "easy" short-term route to competition with the firm across the street or overseas. Overwhelmingly, business chose the second option: to cheapen the work force.

Corporations faced only a few obstacles to this strategy. As the locus of employment shifted to service industries in the postwar years, union membership had dropped from a high of 35 percent of the work force in 1954 to 27 percent in 1970—just over one in four workers. As employers had successfully fought off the spread of unions, barely 1 in 20 service industry jobs were organized.[26] And this meant that organized labor could not hold back the tide of lower wages and reduced benefits for the bulk of the work force.

Public policy both acquiesced to and supported private employers' decisions to cut job standards. Few public laws existed to control private job policy and, despite proposals, few new laws were enacted at either federal or state levels to protect working families in the new environment. The federal minimum wage remained frozen. At both federal and state levels, some public administrators even pursued aggressive programs to cut public wage standards by contracting out jobs and cutting pay and benefits. Additionally, the federal government chose not to alleviate the deep recession in 1981, staking out a hands-off position regarding job creation and full employment. And when federal air traffic control workers protested working conditions, the Reagan administration fired 11,000 of them, sending a clear signal of support to private employers. State and local governments were thus left to develop new policies to address the problems and challenges of the day.

As a result, business faced little effective opposition to its decision to violate the old ground rules. Without legal or community constraints on moving facilities abroad or spinning off work to outside contractors, corporations could pit groups and individual workers against each other and against work forces in Third World countries.

Ramifications of the "Low Wage" Strategy

The low-wage strategy has pulled U.S. wage standards down below those of other countries. No longer in first place, U.S. manufacturing wages today lag behind seven other advanced industrialized countries (table 1.3). And other countries, including Japan, now pay wages nearly equal to those earned by American workers.

But this decline in wages has not translated into productivity growth or an improved international position. Keeping in mind that measures of productivity are often crude, it appears that productivity growth has been cut in half. Before 1973, there was a 2.2 percent annual increase; since then, it has been barely 1 percent a year. For services (for which measurement is even more problematic), output per employee has been flat.[27]

By way of contrast, West Germany, Sweden, and Japan, for example, have chosen to compete not by making their people work harder for less, but by using new technologies to offer higher quality, more diverse goods and services—at lower costs. Their job policies have rewarded their committed, highly trained work force with greater equity and rising income standards, whereas U.S.

**Table 1.3: Manufacturing Wages,
United States vs. Competitors
(Hourly Costs Index, U.S. equals 100)**

	1975	1987
Norway	107	131
Switzerland	96	127
Germany	100	125
Sweden	113	112
Netherlands	103	112
Belgium	101	112
Denmark	99	108
United States	**100**	**100**
Finland	72	97
Austria	68	95
Italy	73	92
France	71	92
Canada	92	89
Japan	48	84
United Kingdom	52	67
Australia	84	64

Source: Patricia Capdevielle, "International Differences in
    Employers' Compensation Costs," *Monthly Labor Review*
    (May 1988): 44.

income standards no longer lead the world and U.S. inequality and
poverty rates far exceed those abroad.

More than a decade into this "low wage" strategy, it is clear that
it was the wrong choice for corporations and families alike. Corporations have gone increasingly into debt to raise new capital, and little
of the improved cash flow has been used for investment in long-
term productive capacity. From 1960 to 1984, the United States
lagged behind other Organization for Economic Cooperation and
Development (OECD) countries in investment in new plants and

equipment. A 1987 Pentagon study found that Japan invests 17 percent of national product; U.S. corporations invest 10 percent.[28]

Instead of investing in the skills, technology, and flexibility needed to compete for new markets with specialized production and services, corporations have spent their money buying and selling other firms. Since 1985 alone, corporations have spent at least $100 billion *per year* on stock buy-backs and acquisitions.[29] The business strategy of expanding by merging rather than innovating means that workers' sacrifices are going to fund "paper entrepreneurship,"[30] from which working families gain nothing. Takeover fights—and restructuring to avoid takeovers—have burdened corporations with high debts and forced sales of valuable assets. The result is more pressure on wages and less money for growth and investment in human and capital resources.

Because of such short-sighted business policies, the United States is failing to reap the benefits of new technology. Although the advent of technology is often blamed for lost jobs, a recent study by the National Academy of Sciences finds that in the United States, dislocation of workers has been caused by the *slow* pace of technological advancement.[31] And experts further criticize U.S. managers for *how* they use technology. For the most part, U.S. corporations still prefer to implement those technologies that emphasize standardized production, with jobs fragmented into small, repetitive tasks. Such technologies are frequently expensive to use and tend to be less flexible in responding to changing consumer demand or technological breakthroughs. For working people, the problems are more monotony, overwork, less control, and less opportunity for advancement.[32]

The global economy and new technology could make possible a great leap forward akin to the nineteenth-century industrial revolution. But critics warn that the low-wage, "old technology" approach favored by most U.S. managers may cause us to miss the opportunity. The failure to invest and innovate, and the preference for mass production, will produce still greater pressures for lowered wages:

Once caution has become habit, new products are designed to fit the existing setup—instead of the setup being refitted to suit the new product; and advances in the technology are limited to small refinements of existing procedures. When product and production technology freeze in this way, the firm is likely to respond to competition from other mass producers by pressing down wages. Sweating, to underscore the point, is the generic response of embattled firms that cannot innovate.[33]

Thus, the U.S. Office of Technology Assessment notes that the nation is at a critical crossroads in the choice of technological change:

Will change come at the expense of workers or will workers themselves be encouraged to change? Will companies assume as some do now, that most workers can fill only narrowly defined roles? If so we're facing a stagnant economy where only the trained elite will benefit while other workers will be used as needed and then displaced. A far brighter scenario comes when business plans on responsive workers and pushes the training required for continuous learning and growth.[34]

Our trading partners have taken advantage of U.S. failure to make the necessary investment in people to use new technology. International competition continues to eat into U.S. markets at home and abroad. Imports continue to rise. Even where prices are equal, U.S. products often lose out because they are of inferior quality. Large trade deficits in the 1980s have replaced the trade surpluses of the 1970s. In less than a decade, the United States has been transformed from the world's largest net creditor to the largest net debtor.

Observers warn that the United States risks losing the vital semiconductor industry. In 1980, the U.S. commanded 60 percent of the world market in this industry; by 1988 its share was down to 40 percent. Why? Because U.S. industry leaders have systematically avoided "long term R&D, personnel training, and long term cooperative relationships," according to a recent study. As a result, employee turnover is high: 20 percent per year, compared with 5 percent in Japan.[35]

The strategy of cheapening jobs has proven to be counterproductive. If corporations reward innovation and hard work with layoffs rather than raises, what motivates employees to take risks and welcome change? If corporate leaders' salaries soar while pay is frozen or cut at the bottom, what happens to the creative energy of those responsible for making the product or delivering the service? And what becomes of the old values of loyalty and hard work? In an economy in which jobs increasingly require mental and social skills rather than sheer muscle power and endurance, the reward, incentive, and protection for working hard is missing.

Even business insiders now worry that the old social contract has not been replaced by any new policies that give people incentives to work productively. As *Business Week* observes:

[Corporate leaders] will soon have to rewrite the social contract they have long had with their employees. For decades it was an unwritten rule in Corporate America that people signed on for the duration and that, the economy willing, the corporation would take care of them. The harsh winds of restructuring have torn this contract to pieces. Corporate loyalty used to be an important factor in getting employees to go the extra mile. With that gone something else has to be devised. . . .

Growth is the most important challenge CEOs face. But how do they rev up machinery that's been so badly battered? Where do they find the creativity to develop new products in a company stripped down to basics? . . . And most of all, how do CEOs motivate workers who have been so thoroughly demoralized?

Right now many CEOs are simply longing for the bygone days. They're hoping that after the big layoffs are over, the old loyalty will return. Don't count on it. Once trust is broken, it isn't easily rebuilt. . . . Fear is no formula for the long haul.[36]

The business press also notes that job performance is suffering among middle management:

> The increased pressure [employers are] putting on middle managers is frequently impairing performance instead of stimulating it. Working scared and tired, many managers simply aren't working well.[37]

International Comparisons, Alternative Choices

Alternatives exist. International competition does not mandate rising poverty, declining income, and growing inequality. To find a more humane and productive strategy for the future, we need only look at other industrialized countries. The most successful competitors, in fact, are those for whom high living standards and improved equity are top priorities.

Income distribution is far more unequal in the United States than it is anywhere else in the industrialized world. In European countries, most families cluster near the middle-income level. In the United States, the vaunted middle class makes up a smaller part of the total population than is the case elsewhere,[38] while many more families—17.1 percent of all people—earn at or below the national average. Even before poverty here began to rise in the 1980s, our nation led eight industrialized countries in the proportion of families living in poverty (table 1.4).

Yet, all industrial countries with high standards of living have faced an identical challenge: how to retain high job standards in the face of increased competition from developing nations with low job standards.

Other countries rejected the low-wage strategy and chose instead to compete on the basis of high quality. Japan, West Germany, France, Sweden, and other industrialized countries increased investment in people, machines, and knowledge—with considerable success.

Table 1.4: Poverty and Inequality in the United States vs. Other Nations (Percent of Population)

	At or Below U.S. Poverty Standard	50 percent or less of Median Income in Country
United States (1979)	12.7	17.1
Australia(1981)	13.2	12.2
Britain(1979)	11.8	9.7
Canada (1981)	7.4	12.6
Norway (1979)	8.6	5.2
Sweden (1981)	5.6	5.3
Switzerland (1982)	5.8	8.5
West Germany (1981)	8.3	5.6

Source: Timothy Smeeding, Barbara Boyle Torrey, and Martin Rein, "Patterns of Income and Poverty: The Economic Status of the Young and the Old in Eight Countries," as cited by Isabel Sawhill, "Poverty and the Underclass," in *Challenge to Leadership: Economic and Social Issues for the New Decade* (Washington, D.C.: Urban Institute, 1988), p. 271, table 7.1.

Japan and Western European countries have achieved productivity growth three to six times higher than that of the United States in recent years, at the same time that they have increased wages to share and reward quality work. Whereas American workers have had to live with stagnant wages in the 1980s, working families in Japan and Western Europe have seen wages, adjusted for inflation, continue to rise each year (table 1.5).

In other countries competition has thus meant both rising living standards *and* more productive work. At the same time, Japan and Western Europe maintain a high wage standard that far surpasses those in developing countries, yet their choice has been to produce either a better product or a specialized one so as to compete

Table 1.5: Wages and Productivity:
United States vs. Japan and Europe (Percent)

	Real Annual Wage Increase 1979-85	Productivity 1979-85	1973-79
United States	0.1	0.5	0.2
Japan	3.6	3.1	3.0
Four major European countries (average)	1.0	1.5	2.1

Source: United Nations, *World Economic Survey* (New York: United Nations, 1987), table VII.4, p. 147.

globally. Their success is now exerting greater pressure on U.S. production of specialized as well as mass-produced goods and services.

Needless to say, international competition and technological change in other industrialized countries have not occurred without pain and disruption. As in the United States, rapid change has rendered skills and industries obsolete almost overnight. There, as here, the challenge has been to forge new policies that will ease the pain and turn change into opportunity. Other countries have met the challenge far better than we have.

Sweden has been remarkably successful at balancing its budget, reducing its trade deficit, bringing unemployment down to 1 percent, increasing living standards across the board, maintaining a comprehensive social welfare system, *and* competing brilliantly in major international manufacturing markets. Kjell-Olof Feldt, Sweden's minister of finance, stated in 1988:

This favorable record has surprised many people. How is such a performance and obvious adaptability possible? After all, the Swedish economy has a very big public sector, unusually high taxes, a generous welfare system, narrow wage differentials and powerful trade unions. . . .

Many Swedes, including myself, are inclined to make the case that small wage differentials and a generous welfare state may actually increase mobility and efficiency in the labor market.[39]

Jan Edgal, vice president of SAF, the Swedish Employers Federation, adds that Swedish employers believe that in an advanced service economy, "we must find ways to motivate people's minds and hearts."[40]

Other nations are proving that pay and benefit levels have increasingly little to do with shifting market shares. Quality counts. Reliability counts. And total costs of production count. But modern production techniques mean that labor costs are a smaller and smaller part of total costs. According to the National Association of Accountants, labor costs now average only 15 percent of the cost of manufacturing production.[41] Similarly, for services produced for international markets, such as finance, insurance, utilities, and telephone, labor costs are but a small part of total outlay.

For those services produced only at the community level, all employers—whether U.S. owned or internationally owned—must hire workers in the same labor market. Hospitals, nursing homes, schools, local banks, hotels, repair shops, stores, and other community or personal services must meet local job and pay standards. As long as standards rise throughout the entire local labor market, no single employer will be disproportionately affected. Labor costs, therefore, will have little to do with competition once a common minimum standard is set. What will count is the *quality* of the service.

Competition based on quality depends on the commitment and skill of the work force and on the organization of work—not on the outlay for wages and benefits. In today's economy this means workers must be willing and able to work creatively and learn new skills or switch careers as technology changes the work process or the nature of work itself. And that means business must renew its commitment to provide quality jobs.

Other industrialized nations have realized that they must use public as well as private policy to improve production in a complex global economy. The United States remains the only nation where independent entrepreneurs are expected to carry the day—an idea MIT Center for Technology researcher Charles H. Ferguson has labeled "Voodoo Competitive Doctrine." "In fact," says Ferguson, "this country faces serious problems that cannot be solved by the unaided efforts of individual entrepreneurs, however ingenious." The decline of vital U.S. industries "reflects the failure of the current terms of competition to provide established corporations the incentives and resources they need for long-term investment, growth and competitiveness."[42]

Unfettered competition among independent competitors, in other words, tends to emphasize the short run over the long run. Each competitor worries that investment will accrue to the benefit of the other. Each worries that his employees will use his expensive training program as a stepping-stone to a new job somewhere else. Each fears that the results of his own research will be used by someone else. In such an environment, it is better not to invent, better not to train, better not to innovate.

Redirecting U.S. Work Policies

Behind the income, inequality, and wage trends that dominate our economy lie job standards that have been lowered, specific job policies that must be turned around, and new issues that must be addressed if we are to make the U.S. economy work for working people in an era of international competition:

—Employers have insisted on wage freezes, cuts, lower tiers, and bonuses in place of increases. The value of the minimum wage is down. Higher-wage jobs have been eliminated as production has shifted to low-wage countries.

—Employers are abandoning their former commitment to provide health insurance and pensions.

—More people have been pushed to the margins of the work force through the creation of a second tier of part-time, temporary, and contracted jobs that carry neither benefits, nor advancement opportunities, nor job security. The Conference Board estimates one-quarter of all jobs are now outside core employment.

—More two-wage earner families and more women in the work force create new tensions and increase the need for flexible leave policies, dependent care, and pay equity.

—The lack of a comprehensive national jobs policy has led to an underinvestment in training and education.

—Service employment contains many "hidden" hazards, requiring a new look at our current health and safety standards.

Taken together, these policies and the lack of standards appropriate to our new economy allow employers to shift costs out of the corporate budget and onto the shoulders of working families.

Reduced job standards have pulled down families and the economy. Slow growth, loss of markets, and stagnant productivity are the direct outcome of the failure to link corporate success with rising living standards. Relying on corporations to shape job policy—in the absence of an organized work force—is no longer sufficient. If the marketplace alone will not move corporations to make the right choices for our nation and develop the full potential of the work force, then public policy must take the lead. It is time for a change.

The major failure of American business is seeing the employee as part of the problem, instead of as part of the solution.

—Tom Peters, co-author of
In Search of Excellence, in an interview
with *U.S. News and World Report*, July 15, 1985.

In this age of automation, the labor-cost fetish is an anachronism that has been sapping U.S. competitiveness by diverting attention from more crucial issues. . . .
—*Business Week*, editorial, June 13, 1988.

The average service worker is far worse off than workers in manufacturing, mining, or construction. Which, of course, doesn't mean that we should, or could, curtail the growth of services, but rather that we must reorganize how service jobs are performed and remunerated.
—Bennett Harrison, Massachusetts
Institute of Technology, in an
address to the Conference on Solutions
for the New Workforce, Washington, DC.

You know, when I became active in Justice for Janitors, they put me off in an area by myself. At first they told me it was because I do such good work. Then they told me the truth. Being alone I get a chance to think. There are a lot of old people up there, working with me. I think about this one little old woman; it looks like her leg is just going to burst. And then I think of my grandson. . .what it's going to be like for him. That makes me want to fight harder.

—Mary Jenkins, cleaner in Atlanta.

Chapter 2:
Declining Pay

Mary Jenkins cleans office high-rises in downtown Atlanta. Every night she cleans the equivalent of 12 single-family homes. Some nights she does it on an empty stomach: her wages are so low she can't always afford to buy enough food for herself and the 5-year-old grandson she's raising. And Mary is not alone. Most workers earned less than $12,500 in 1987—counting full and part-time workers.[1] Hourly wages adjusted for inflation are down 7 percent since the early 1970s. Work hours have been cut, too: weekly pay has plummeted 15 percent.[2]

Working people once believed that a fair day's work would receive a fair day's pay. Today more and more people wonder whether the days of partnership with industry are gone along with the American dream of a better tomorrow.

We have already noted the corporate decision to make the United States get by on lower wages. Five major job policies together have contributed to this effort: wage reduction and concession bargaining, elimination of high-wage jobs and the concomitant increase in low-wage jobs, reduction in the value of the minimum wage, sex and race discrimination, and antiunion activity. All five strategies have lowered the living standards of low- and middle-income families while leaving those at the top freer to set their own wages and to restructure jobs and industries at will.

Wage Reduction and Concession Bargaining

For most of the 1970s, high inflation and rising unemployment undercut wage advances. Earning power was stagnant or down in manufacturing and service industries alike. For most people, success meant hanging on.

The deep recession of 1981 spurred a new trend toward outright reductions in pay. Under the guise of regaining a competitive advantage, manufacturing industries started the trend, forcing union and nonunion employees to choose either pay cuts or layoffs and plant closures. (Even after winning steep concessions, many corporations moved or closed plants, anyway.)

Six years of economic recovery (1983-88) have not ended the "concession" trend. Today, profitable and endangered employers alike demand reduced pay standards in union negotiations and cut pay unilaterally for unorganized workers. In 1987, with its booming economy, 4 percent of major union contracts still contained across-the-board pay reductions, and public and private employers have stepped up efforts to contract out work to business service firms who usually pay substandard wages. Pay freezes eroded income in another 11 percent of all major union contracts, and as inflation raises the cost of living by 3-4 percent per year, wage freezes are effectively cutting pay by the same percentage (table 2.1).

Moreover, two new pay policies—two-tiered wage systems and bonuses or lump-sum payments in lieu of wage increases—have also cut pay standards. One in 10 union contracts now has a two-tiered pay scale: the top tier is reserved for employees hired before some specified date; the bottom is for all new hires. Two workers with only a day's difference in tenure can earn dramatically different pay for the same work. And since women, minorities, and young workers are the most likely "new hires" in higher-wage industries, two-tiered systems constitute a discriminatory system.

So far, however, the courts have found them to be within legal bounds.

Table 2.1:
Wage Concessions Among Unionized Workers, 1987

	Percent
Wage cuts	4.0[a]
Wage freeze	11.0[a]
Two tiers	
Nonconstruction	9.0[b]
Nonmanufacturing	12.0[b]
Wage bonus	55.0[c]

[a]Percent of all workers covered by contracts with 1,000 employees or more.
[b]Percent of contracts.
Sources: BLS, "News Release USDL 88-33," 26 January 1988, p., table 2; Bureau of National Affairs (hereafter BNA), *Changing Pay Practices: New Developments in Employee Compensation*, a BNA Special Report (Washington, D.C.: BNA, 1988), p. A-4; BNA, *Daily Labor Report* (from BLS statistics), 27 January 1988, p. B-9.

It is worth noting that even profitable corporations have instituted two-tiered wage systems. In 1986, Kaiser Permanente Health Plan, a $4 billion health care system, demanded a 35 percent cut in pay and a permanent second tier for 10,000 Northern California health workers who are represented by SEIU. Kaiser did not cite financial distress as the reason for the cutbacks; in fact, corporate profits were at record highs, the plan was expanding, and with 70 percent of all patients under 65, Kaiser had a near monopoly in the area. Rather, Kaiser simply asserted that it was time for a "new policy." The cut brought starting pay below $16,000 per year. New hires were required to work on high-pressure teams for almost $3,000 per year less than their co-workers, and the bottom tier would never be able to catch up to the more senior workers.

After a 10-week strike, employees cut the tier differential to 15 percent, but they were unable to kill the concept entirely. Less than a year into the new system, however, Kaiser eliminated the tier for some employees, citing problems with morale and hiring difficulties.

In fact, many companies have found that a two-tiered system creates conflicts among workers and erodes quality and productivity, costs that often outweigh any short-term gains. Noting the existence of fewer new two-tiered systems in recent years, The Conference Board reported that corporations are having second thoughts: 'Increased resentment does not help a corporation increase its productivity, quality, or profits.'[3]

The payment of lump-sum bonuses in lieu of raises is perhaps more insidious because the erosion in pay standards is less visible. Starting in manufacturing, the practice has spread rapidly across service industries as well. Such payments affected 55 percent of all workers and 32 percent of collective bargaining contracts in 1987.[4]

Lump-sum payments amount to wage freezes: they give people extra money for one year only. The next year, the frozen wage base is still in effect pending another "lump," which sometimes may not be granted for years—especially in a multiyear contract. An SEIU study found that after six years, earning power would drop by 11 percent if employees were granted only periodic bonus payments instead of wage increases. The impact on pensions is even more severe. Bonuses aren't counted into pension earnings, and with wages remaining flat instead of increasing, a bonus system would result in a 16 percent loss of pension benefits for a retiring employee.[5] With the value of pensions already falling (see chap. 5), the lump-sum fad is a major threat to retirement security.

Elimination of High-Wage Jobs, Increase in Low-Wage Jobs

Employers threaten that unless workers accept deep wage cuts, they will lose their jobs. But then they renege on the bargain and cut jobs anyway. Since 1979 manufacturing firms have cut 2 million jobs.[6] And six years into an economic recovery, it is clear that this job loss is not recession based but is instead a permanent fact of life in our current economy.

The lost jobs paid $21,000 per year—considerably above the national average of $12,500.[7] In contrast, new job growth has occurred at the other end of the payscale, as an estimated 44 percent of all new jobs created between 1979 and 1985 paid $7,400 or less.[8] In addition, by 1985 one in three new full-time jobs paid less than $11,184 per year, which is below the poverty line for a family of four. By contrast, less than 14 percent of all full-time jobs in the early 1970s paid so little, after adjustment for inflation.[9] And a look at the pay of the fastest growing and declining jobs tells the same story. Five of the top 10 *expanding* jobs pay below poverty wages; only two of the top ten *declining* jobs pay poverty wages (figure 2.1).

Figure 2.1: Projected Job Growth and Decline, 1986-2000

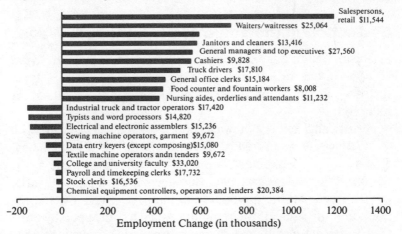

* Excludes agricultural and private household occupations, and occupations employing under 75,000 workers.

Source: G.T. Silvestri and J.M. Lukasiewicz, "A Look at Occupational Employment Trends to the Year 2000," *Monthly Labor* (September 1987), tables 3 and 5; Bureau of Labor Statistics, unpublished median earnings data; Bureau of the Census, *Money Income and Poverty Status in the United States: 1987,* (Washington, D.C.: U.S. GPO, 198), table A-1.

Wages for many of the jobs of the future pay poverty wages today. One in four new custodians earns the minimum wage; half earn less than $4 an hour. Worse, many new jobs offer short hours on top of low wages, forcing workers to patch together a minimal income with several part-time jobs. As figure 2.1 indicates, often it is the type of industry—not the type of work or the skills required—that determines how much a job will pay. But throughout the nation, the low pay standard set by the service industries is fast becoming the norm for all firms as the higher manufacturing standard fades away.

Massive business restructuring—through mergers, takeovers, and spinoffs—has contributed to the loss of higher-paid manufacturing jobs. The Conference Board estimates that restructuring disrupted the lives of some 40 million people between 1985 and 1988 alone.[10] Entire communities have seen good, secure jobs disappear overnight or come under new management with lower pay and benefit scales.

Reduction in the Value of the Minimum Wage

The minimum wage determines the standard of living for 6-1/2 million workers, nearly 7 percent of the labor force. It also sets the scale for the 5.4 million whose wages hover within 50 cents of the minimum.[11]

Historically, minimum wage policy sought to keep up with average hourly wage trends. The minimum was set at or near 50 percent of the average. The goal was to bring people at the bottom closer to average pay. But since 1981, thanks to inflation, a freeze on the national minimum wage has lowered the floor, and the value of the minimum wage has dropped by more than 30 percent. A full-time minimum-wage worker earning $6,834 doesn't make enough to keep a family out of poverty. And two full-time workers with two children could work year-round and still be unable to afford the bare necessities: food, clothing, rent, and utilities.

The declining minimum wage has encouraged employers to exploit people rather than use machines to perform repetitive or dangerous tasks. Not surprisingly, minimum wage jobs are characterized by high turnover, high absenteeism, and little upward mobility. Rather than tapping the maximum human potential, rock-bottom pay wastes people.

For example, according to a 1985-86 California health care facilities report, California's nursing home industry is among the beneficiaries of a declining minimum wage. Aides work full time and earn less than $7,000 per year with no benefits. But the average annual turnover rate among such workers is 99 percent, and 45 percent of staff stay less than a year. Patients barely learn the names of their caretakers, and staff receive little more information on their patients. And each year, violations of minimum care standards persist as low quality goes hand in hand with low pay.[12]

As workers at the bottom find it harder and harder to survive, some states, along with the District of Columbia, are leading the way in raising the minimum wage. Although business contends that such an increase will result in job loss, little evidence exists in these areas to support that prediction.

Sex and Race Discrimination

Despite revolutionary change in the jobs people do, discrimination on the basis of sex and race has been carried from the old job hierarchy into the new. Women still do not perform many of the jobs men do, nor do minorities perform many of the jobs whites do. And female- and minority-dominated jobs pay less.

Achieving an equal sex mix across jobs would require two out of three people to change jobs. Affirmative action programs that aim to integrate the work force have only taken the edge off discriminatory recruitment, training, and career policies. And segregation has limited the application of laws guaranteeing equal pay for equal work.

Despite increasingly similar work patterns and jobs requiring comparable skill, effort, and responsibility, pay inequity remains strong between men and women. For decades, the pay gap between average male and female earnings stood at 59 percent. (For every dollar paid to men, women took home only 59 cents.) Women now make 65 percent as much as men, but that improvement is due in part to a decline in men's wages.[13]

The pay gap persists regardless of work history. A recent Census Bureau study compared male and female earnings for workers with no interruptions in their work lives and found that women still earn only 69 percent of male hourly wages. The gap persists even when women enter traditionally male occupations. Female attorneys, for example, earn only 63 percent as much as their male counterparts.[14] And the gap widens when we compare the earnings (including full and part-time income) of all women and all men workers, because women work part time more often than men and earn just 44.7 percent of what men earn.

Figure 2.2: Pay Inequity in San Francisco

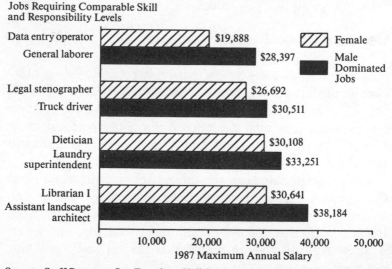

Jobs Requiring Comparable Skill
and Responsibility Levels

Data entry operator — $19,888 — Female
General laborer — $28,397 — Male Dominated Jobs
Legal stenographer — $26,692
Truck driver — $30,511
Dietician — $30,108
Laundry superintendent — $33,251
Librarian I — $30,641
Assistant landscape architect — $38,184

0   10,000   20,000   30,000   40,000   50,000
1987 Maximum Annual Salary

Source: Staff Report to San Francisco Civil Service Commission, Jan., 1987.

The industry and location of jobs explain only part of the inequity. Numerous studies of specific employers have found that employers who hire both men and women and still maintain job segregation pay less for female-dominated jobs, regardless of job requirements. One such study is illustrated in figure 2.2, which shows average earnings of city workers in San Francisco in 1987. Jobs dominated by women paid less up and down the job hierarchy than did jobs held predominantly by men. Revelation of a persistent bias against female-dominated jobs in San Francisco led to a referendum campaign in which workers mobilized voters to end pay inequity. The result was $35.4 million in pay equity adjustments.

Many state and city unions and a few private sector unions have fought successful battles for pay equity across the country. Working with employers and legislators, they have slowly won major changes in pay plans. Law suits are pending that would bring fair pay to thousands more. Yet the federal government has failed to act, and pay inequity remains the norm for most workers.

Antiunion Activity

The success of U.S. employers in lowering wage standards is due in large part to the lack of unionization among workers. Confronted with strong employer opposition, the proportion of organized workers has been declining for 30 years. New organizing has been unable to make up for the loss of unionized manufacturing jobs to Third World countries and the movement of unionized jobs to nonunion communities. Consequently, unionization in this country lags far behind that in most advanced industrialized countries (table 2.2).

The United States stands alone among industrialized countries in its failure to give workers a collective voice through labor unions. By the 1980s, U.S. unions represented only one in every five employed men and women. The only industries in which more than 30 percent of the workers were organized were public utilities, transportation, and government, while fewer than 10 percent of workers in the rapidly growing private service sector were unionized. In stark contrast, by 1982 Japan—with the lowest rate of unionization among industrialized countries other than the United States— saw one-third of its labor force organized. And since 1982, the proportion of organized workers abroad has increased.[15]

Table 2.2:
Unionization Among Selected Industrialized Countries (Percentage of Nonagricultural Work Force Organized)

Sweden	92
Denmark	81
United Kingdom	59
Australia	57
Netherlands	46
Germany	44
Canada	37
Switzerland	36
Japan	33
United States	**17.3-19.4**[b]

Notes: [a] Data for the United States alone are from 1987; all other data are from 1982.

[b]Percentages are adjusted for nonagricultural workers. The range represents union membership compared with representation.

Sources: BLS, "Union Membership in 1987," 22 January 1988; unpublished data from the Labor Department, 1982, as cited in Thomas Byrne Edsall, *The New Politics of Inequality* (New York: Norton, 1984), p. 256.

The U.S. decline in unionization is no accident of history. Since the late 1960s, corporate leaders have fought to keep unions out of new industries, engaging in firings, harassment, and campaigns whenever there was even the hint of organizing; and weak labor laws and lax enforcement have facilitated their efforts. In 1978, business leaders pulled out all the stops to defeat a labor law reform bill that would merely have brought U.S. labor law nearer to Canadian standards.[16]

But perhaps most telling are official statistics that detail the massive employer violations of labor laws. According to the National Labor Relations Board (NLRB), the annual number of union elections between 1970 and 1980 remained almost constant at about 8,000. But the total number of unfair charges increased threefold; the number of workers reinstated after having been illegally fired increased fourfold; the number of workers receiving compensatory awards for unfair labor practices more than doubled; and the cash amount of the awards went up by a factor of 15 (table 2.3).

Table 2.3: Employer Violations of Labor Laws

	1970	1980
Number of elections	8,074	8,198
Number of unfair charges filed against employers	13,601	31,281
Number of workers reinstated	2,723	8,592
Number of workers awarded back pay	6,828	15,566
Amount of back pay awarded	$2.7 mil	$31.1 mil

Source: Thomas Byrne Edsall, *The New Politics of Inequality* (New York: Norton, 1984), based on NLRB annual reports.

The hospital industry illustrates both the efforts of employers to keep workers unorganized as well as the acquiesence of public policymakers. After the National Labor Relations Act (NLRA) was extended to nonprofit hospitals in 1974, hospital journals immediately began running articles advising administrators on how to remain "union free." One hospital after another hired a new brand of management consultant—the "union buster"—to break collective momentum among workers. Employers then passed on the cost of these consultants to the taxpayers, billing public health programs for most of what they called "increased management services." By 1980, the annual cost of consultant expenses among hospitals had reached an estimated $30 million per year.[17] Finally, in 1981, Congress prohibited the use of public funds to pay for antiunion activities.

But the antiunion strategy has so far been successful. By 1987, union membership totaled just over 17 percent of all wage and salaried employees.[18] Thomas Edsall, a reporter for the *Washington Post*, notes that this success has exerted a significant push toward a "new politics of inequality." Of the union, he writes,

> there exists in no Western democracy any other major organization cutting across racial and ethnic lines that can defend progressive distributional policies of both taxation and spending. In this context, the decline of organized labor in the United States takes on new and significant meaning for the formulation of economic policy.[19]

Individual workers and their families are unlikely to be able to reverse the trends toward rising inequality and declining income on their own. Thus, the erosion of the only organized institution dedicated to the interests of working people has profound implications for U.S. political democracy, as well as for our position in the world economy.

Stress and Low Morale: The Cost of Low-Wage Corporate Policies

Aggressive attacks on wages, the elimination of high-wage jobs, two-tiered pay scales, pay discrimination, and the decline of the minimum wage have all taken a toll on employees. Stress, insecurity, and the struggle to make ends meet have reduced workers' ability to get the job done and pulled worker morale to new lows. According to a 1987 survey, most managers notice that workers show less interest in extra hours, less dedication to their work, and poorer attendance and punctuality.[20]

Stress at work has reached epidemic proportions.

In the past, stress was viewed as a problem of the individual employee. But now it's at the organizational level. The stress-point between the employee and the company results from the change in part of the informal employment agreement between both parties. According to this (old) understanding, the employee will give time, skill, dedication to organizational goals and loyalty in return for employment security, promotion, opportunities and compensation increases.[21]

Stress. From the corner office to the factory floor, it's epidemic in U.S. business. . . . Signs are everywhere. Employees drink to excess and slip disastrously in their performance. They erupt into fits of uncontrollable rage at work and abuse their families at home. . . . The conditions that put employees into the pressure cooker are fairly constant: fear of job loss, work overload, lack of control over one's work, nonsupportive supervisors or co-workers, limited job opportunities, conflict and uncertainty. What's changing is that those conditions are now the rule, not the exception. The rate of major depression is rising among those born since 1940, as is the rate of suicide among those born since 1930.[22]

Increased stress at work is now costing an estimated $150 billion annually in sickness and disability payments.[23] Yet researchers have only begun to document such rising trends as increased alcoholism, drug abuse, and battered families—all by-products of stress.

Stress and low morale hurt in the area of international competition as well. In an era when increased productivity—the ability to produce more with fewer resources—requires more worker involvement in the process, the growing belief that a fair day's work will not result in a fair day's pay threatens U.S. productivity. A 1988 study of American, European, and Japanese workers concluded that "the American commitment to the work ethic may be a thing of the past."[24] News media accounts of new millionaires and queues for high-priced Mercedes automobiles only heighten the message that some people matter and others don't anymore. And the breakdown in apparent rewards for work shows up in slower U.S. economic growth, greater loss of industries, higher trade deficits, and the like. Thus, stress and low morale cannot help but impair our ability to compete in the global economy.

The Task at Hand

Cutting labor costs has too often been the only competitive strategy pursued by U.S. managers. Redesign of work and investment in both equipment and the work force have all fallen by the wayside. To now direct corporate energies toward productive rather than destructive ends, we must take cheap labor and discrimination out of the equation. Once businesses in every industry are required to pay decent wages across industries, domestic competition will hinge on the quality of products and performance, not on the exploitation of workers. The past has shown that even low-wage employers can survive higher pay standards, as long as competition based on wages is prohibited.

The vivid contrast between the pay of custodians in New York and those in Washington, D.C., is a case in point. In both cities the real estate industry is large and powerful. In both cities, cleaning wages make up only a small part of rents paid by building tenants. But in Washington, D.C., nonunion pay is set building by building. Wages are at the minimum; there are no benefits; and each job is half time, forcing the work force to juggle multiple jobs. By contrast, in New York, master union contracts cover all major building owners and all cleaning contracts throughout the city, setting pay standards for 65,000 workers. New York custodians earn $11.29 per hour, with full benefits and full-time work. What makes the difference between decent wages in New York and poverty in Washington, D.C., is an agreement by the New York real estate industry as a whole to raise the standard.

We must recognize that our goal is not to compete with the wage rates existing in countries like Singapore or Taiwan. The United States should not aspire to standards as low as those maintained in less developed countries. Rather, our answer to competition and growth lies in policies that maintain and improve upon our standard of living. Such policies will benefit our workers and our families as well as our economy. The health and well-being of our people and our nation are inextricable.

To reverse low and discriminatory wages, the first steps are simple: raise pay at the bottom and make pay equity the law. But to enable workers and their families to affect pay policy, we must go further. We must enact legislation that limits or controls corporations seeking to relocate or to restructure without regard for the surrounding community and that requires advanced notice and community participation in plant closing decisions. And we must encourage industry development and long-term investments that are aimed at raising both living standards and production. Finally, labor law reform is an essential adjunct of these new policies. A collective voice gives working people input into wage policies, making them part of the process rather than subject to the whim of change. Pressure at the roots remains the most direct mechanism for maintaining balance and a sense of equity in the society.

Solutions

The solutions, detailed below, lie in the hands of both the federal government and the private sector. As can be seen, some have already been successfully implemented. However, much more must be done before we can reverse the destructive low-wage trends of the last decade.

—*Restoration of the minimum wage.* Restoring the minimum wage and indexing future increases to the average wage will raise millions out of poverty and stimulate the economy.

Eleven states have already acted to raise their own minimums; 4 more have legislation pending. But federal action is necessary to avoid pitting states against one another.

—*Enactment of equity policies.* Pay equity laws and initiatives enacted by 20 states require employers to apply a single pay standard to jobs requiring comparable skill, effort, and responsibility, thereby eliminating pay disparities based on sex, race, or ethnic background. Here again, federal legislation is needed to cover federal employees and make discrimination among comparable jobs illegal for public as well as private employers throughout the country.

—*Pay equity negotiations.* In the absence of pay equity legislation, however, unions negotiate settlements. Standard evaluation methods, as well as systems developed for particular workplace, have effectively reduced wage inequities. So far, such efforts have been implemented primarily in the public sector.

—*Laws that limit or control company relocation or restructuring and require advance notice of closures.* The United States, alone among industrialized countries, lacks strong requirements and controls on employers seeking to lay-off workers, move operations, or close down altogether. Congress only recently (July 1988) passed federal legislation requiring 60 days advance notification. We must follow the lead of other countries and some states in requiring early worker input and funds for severance pay, retraining, and placement in the event of closure or major restructuring. Sweden, for example, requires employers who plan any major change in operations to disclose information to employees and the community. West Germany requires workers to be represented on corporate boards. And both countries require corporations to help workers maintain living standards in the event that corporate decisions ultimately result in job loss. Federal action is needed in the United States to keep employers from playing off one community against another and to make employers bear at least some of the costs of dislocation.

—*Economic development plans that support higher-wage jobs.* Public investment programs and community planning activities should include the type, mix, and quality of jobs as criteria for investment. Support should focus on those projects and work design likely to create higher skill demands and support higher pay.

—*Model programs that redesign work.* Technology can be used to design highly creative tasks or highly routinized ones, to eliminate low-skill jobs or proliferate them. Public employers should provide experimental models to point the way for the private sector. Certain private employers have also developed model jobs as a result of union contracts that require worker participation in work design (see chap. 6).

—*Labor law reform that enables the new work force to organize.* The NLRA currently allows long delays between the time workers decide to organize and the achievement of a union contract. Penalties against employers who retaliate illegally for union activity are minimal, and penalties against employers who refuse to agree on a first contract are virtually nonexistent. In Canada, where labor laws impose significant penalties, expedite elections, and bar the use of strike breakers, nearly 50 percent of all workers were organized by 1988.

Setting benefit standards; reducing the exploitation of people working at the "margins" of full-time work; and pursuing education, training, and job initiatives would further support the goal of moving the domestic and international payscale up. Such policies will be discussed in subsequent chapters.

Case Studies

Voters Say "Yes" to Pay Equity in San Francisco

November 1986 was the first time pay equity was won at the polls, and it won big—by 61 percent. The place was San Francisco, where three SEIU locals (790, 535, and 250) put a measure on the ballot to raise pay for city workers in jobs held predominantly by women and minorities. As a result, more than 11,000 employees—most of them clerical, library, cafeteria, and custodial workers—received pay equity adjustments of 9.5 percent over two years. Adjustments received totaled $35.4 million.

The process began in 1981, when the mayor and the Board of Supervisors approved a study of the city wage scale. "The study documented what the union already knew—that the wages of women and minorities lagged far behind those of white men," says Margaret Butz, deputy director of SEIU Local 790 in San Francisco. The city agreed to allocate $19.5 million for pay equity adjustments if a legal way could be found. But there could be no bargaining over how exactly to allocate funds allotted for adjustments: in San Francisco, public employees cannot legally bargain over wages.

After some backsliding by the mayor, the union and city attorneys eventually settled on a public referendum as the required legal mechanism. Proposition H was supported by a coalition of public employee unions, women, minority, and other community groups.

"To my knowledge," says Butz, "this was the first jurisdiction to affirm pay equity at the polls. The issue of pay equity goes beyond the workplace. There's tremendous support out there for the concept that women and minority workers must be paid what they deserve."

Pay Equity in the State of Oregon

In 1985, a task force established by the Oregon state legislature declared that wages in female-dominated state jobs were far less than those in male-dominated jobs. University secretaries, for example, earned $200 less per week than university groundskeepers; day care workers on the university campus earned $100 less per week than technicians who took care of laboratory rats.

The legislature responded to these findings by passing a bill mandating $5 million in immediate wage adjustments and further study to produce a more comprehensive pay equity plan.

Then the governor vetoed the bill.

"At this point," says Margaret Hallock, past economist for the Oregon Public Employees Union/SEIU Local 503 and chair of the state task force on pay equity, "the union decided we had to organize support among state workers. We went from workplace to workplace, educating, holding rallies and meetings. We held pay equity testimonials for state legislators. We hosted 'pie equity' days in which we sold pies to women for $1 and to men for 59 cents. We held lobby days, a candlelight vigil, and a statewide women's conference on pay equity."

With its newly mobilized troops, the union turned to political action, working hard to elect a new governor who had pledged support for pay equity. His first budget called for $22.6 million in pay equity adjustments for state employees. It passed the state legislature in June of 1987.

"Even then our battle was not over," says Hallock. "The state wanted to make a one-time adjustment. We wanted to upgrade the classifications of the lowest-grade employees so that the changes would be permanent."

The pay equity disagreement and other contract conflicts propeled the union into a nine-day strike in fall 1987. By the end of the strike, the union had won most of what it wanted on the pay equity issue. On October 1, 1987, over 5,500 state workers received an average pay equity increase of $100 per month—a total of $22.6 million statewide. Adjustments of 5 to 10 percent went to the lowest-paid state employees, 90 percent of whom were women in clerical, food service, and health care jobs.

I used to work for the city transit authority. I earned $11.40 an hour, had a pension and health plan, and received overtime pay. Then I hurt my back and had to stop working for two years. When I went back, I got a job with a big building contractor. I wanted full-time work, but they told me I'd have to start part time. So now I work 20 hours a week. I earn $4.25 an hour. No pension, no health care coverage, no sick days, no vacation time, no paid overtime. I had to take a second part-time job putting inserts in newspapers. I don't get any benefits from that job, either.

—Arthur Ward, building service worker,
Washington, D.C.

We hire a lot of nurses from a temporary agency. They don't know the doctors, can't read their writing, don't know the procedures, or where we keep the medicine and supplies. It's unsafe for the patients and disruptive for the regular nurses. We end up doing much of their work anyway.

—Bridget O'Neill, nurse at a
community hospital in La Plata, Md.

If corporate executives think using contingent workers is going to be a free lunch, they are going to be surprised....The quality and the motivating issues are the two Achilles' heels.
—Richard Belous, economist, The Conference Board,
in an interview in the *Wall Street Journal*, April 12, 1988.

Chapter 3:
The Contingent Work Force: Part-Time, Temporary, and Contract Workers

Most employed Americans work full time for a single employer. But in the past decade, another kind of work has grown dramatically. "We're at the beginning of a fundamental change in employment practices," says Eli Ginzberg of Columbia University. "We used to hire, and now we don't want to hire people at all, except on a contractual basis."

Thirty-five million people, almost one-third of the work force, now make their living as part-time, temporary, or contract employees. Some observers call them "contingent" workers because their employment is contingent upon daily, weekly, or seasonal renewal. Others term them "marginal" workers because they exist at the margins of employment and economic security. *Fortune* magazine calls them the "disposable" work force.[1]

The growth of the contingent work force has largely been a phenomenon of the 1980s (table 3.1). A decade of corporate restructuring in the name of competition, flexibility, and short- term profits struck a powerful blow at full-time employment and wage and benefit standards. At first, it was the recession of 1981 that fueled the push toward contingent workers. But even during the period of recovery and economic expansion that followed, companies continued to hire on a part-time or temporary basis rather than create new permanent positions. Half of all new jobs in the 1980s were filled by part-time or temporary employees.[2]

Table 3.1: Growth of the Contingent Work Force

	(millions of workers)		Percent
	1980	1988	Change
Part-time	14.3	20.0	40.0
Temporary	0.6	1.3	117.0
Business services	2.5	4.0	60.0
Self-employed	8.4	9.8	16.7
Total contingent work force	25.8	35.1	36.0
Total civilian work force	105.5	120.9	14.6

Note: The term *temporary* includes only those workers hired through agencies, not the thousands of temporary employees hired directly by public and private sector employers. *Business services* workers include employees working on contract to supply services such as cleaning, guarding, or data processing to business.

Sources: BLS, *Labor Force Statistics Derived from the Current Population Survey: A Databook*, September 1982, tables A-17 and A-4 (vol 1), table D-10 (vol. 2); BLS, *Supplement to Employment and Earnings*, July 1984, p. 309; BLS, *Employment and Earnings*, May 1988, tables A-35 and B-2.

Contingent workers are drawn primarily from groups at the bottom of the employment hierarchy—women, minorities, the young, and the old. In fact, while women comprise only 45 percent of the total labor force, they comprise 64 percent of all temporary workers and 65 percent of workers who are employed part time. Most contingent workers hold low-level retail, clerical, and service jobs. But the trend has affected every industry and level. Accountants, engineers, nurses, and even doctors and managers now work on a contract basis.

If employers are looking for a flexible work force, some members of the new work force are in turn looking for flexible work. Part-time, seasonal, or temporary jobs fit the needs of those who must meet family responsibilities, go to school, or combine work with partial retirement, or those who are financially able to work part time (figure 3.1).

Figure 3.1: Where Contingent Workers Are Employed

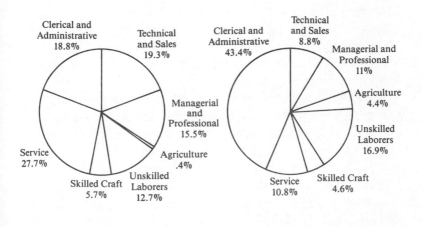

Part-Time

Temporaries

Source: BLS, *Employment and Earnings,*
April 1988.

Source: *Monthly Labor Review,*
November 1986.

But many who find themselves in today's contingent work force are not there by choice. Millions of part-time and temporary employees are unable to find the permanent, full-time jobs they need to support their families. Among part-time workers, those who would prefer full-time jobs ('involuntary part-time workers") are growing twice as fast as those working part-time by choice.[3] Moonlighting is up, as 5.7 million workers piece together several marginal jobs to make ends meet.[4]

The need for flexibility drives some companies to downgrade full-time permanent positions into contingent jobs. But in an era when employers spend an average of one-quarter of total employee compensation on benefits, many create part-time positions simply to escape these costs.[5] A community hospital in Prestonburg, Ky., for example, limits hospital workers to 39 hours per week, classifies them as part-timers, and pays them no benefits. Some clerical workers at Cuyahoga Community College who work 40 hours a week are officially called "part-time" and paid at part-time wage and benefit rates. Los Angeles County classifies 10,000 workers as "temporary" employees. They do the same work as permanent employees—sometimes for decades—but receive lower wages and no benefits. Even the federal government has gotten into the act. More than 300,000 of its employees now work up to four years as temporaries without benefits.

A marginal work force may be flexible, and it may be cheap. But for employers who are looking for higher productivity or quality, contingent workers are not the answer. Many employers find that the less they give to a worker—in the form of wages, benefits, and working conditions—the less hard work and quality performance they can expect to get back in return. "There's no question that you get greater productivity out of a permanent employee," says Jim Schmidt, director of Human Resources at Apple Computer, where temporary employment has increased from 2 to 17 percent since 1985.[6] Moreover, as business magazines have begun to acknowledge, "using temps poses dangers, in particular a threat to productivity."[7] Managers at Corroon and Black, a large insurance brokerage firm, report a bitter experience in which a temporary worker hired to stuff envelopes dumped 80,000 of them into a freight elevator, knowing she'd be long gone before her misdeed was discovered.[8] And for their part, workers who need flexible schedules are poorly served by part-time and temporary positions that offer little security, equity, financial rewards, or advancement opportunity.

Problems for Part-Time and Temporary Workers

In addition to earning only 60 percent of the average full-timer's hourly wage,[9] most part-timers do not receive basic benefits, either from their employers or from public programs. The same is true of temporaries. Employers save an average of 15.4 percent of payroll costs on benefits by hiring part-time and temporary workers; they save an additional 8.6 percent by hiring workers on contract (table 3.2).

—*Health insurance.* Less than one-fourth of part-time workers receive health coverage on the job, whereas three-quarters of all full-time employees do.[10] Only one in four temporary agencies offers workers the opportunity to participate in a health insurance plan.[11] And many temps cannot use the benefits even when they are offered: some do not put in enough hours with one agency to qualify for the benefits; others cannot afford the high copayments.

—*Pensions.* Federal law requires employers who provide pensions to cover all employees working more than 1,000 hours per year. Many temporary and part-time workers do not work this many hours. Many leave their employers long before they become vested (eligible for contributions). As a result, fewer than one in four part-time workers are members of a pension plan and only 15 percent will ever see any benefits.[12] As for temps, only 2 percent of agencies offer pension plans. Compare these statistics with the fact that over half of all full-time workers participate in a pension plan.[13]

—*Other benefits.* Most part-time and temporary workers also miss out on such benefits as sick leave, vacation leave, disability pay, parental leave, and job training. Independent consultants and employees working on contract are even worse off; their employers are not required to contribute to Social Security or workers' compensation, nor are they covered by minimum wage, health and safety regulations, or other labor protections.

Table 3.2:
Employer Savings with a Contingent Work Force

	Employee Benefits As a Percent of Payroll
Benefit Costs Saved with Part-time And Temporary Workers	
Insurance: life, health	5.6
Pensions	2.8
Vacations, sick leave, parental leave, holidays, lunch breaks, etc.	7.0
Subtotal	15.4
Benefit Costs Saved with Independent Contractors	
Social Security	5.9
Unemployment compensation	1.0
Workers' compensation	1.7
Subtotal	8.6
Total	24.0

Source: BLS, "Employer Costs for Employee Compensation: March 1988," 16 June 1988.

Contingent workers fall outside the boundaries of other public and private programs, as well. Most do not qualify for unemployment compensation between jobs. And only six states pay unemployment compensation to men and women who are actively looking for part-time work.

Nor do current labor laws provide them with adequate protection. In the public sector, for example, some state labor laws exclude temporary workers from bargaining units; others are vague about the rights of part-time employees. In the private sector, part-time and temporary workers who want to be included in bargaining units often must fight time-consuming legal battles. Given the long delays allowed by the law, holding a union election or negotiating a first contract can take years. Marginal workers, with their short-term job tenure, find it nearly impossible to organize.

For the most part, contingent workers are also excluded from career ladders. Affirmative action strategies that encourage upward mobility for women and minorities *within* a firm do not work when internal career ladders have broken down. Contract and temporary workers are not officially employees; they are not included in affirmative action plans. Some firms have even made a policy of not hiring temporary employees into permanent slots so as to maintain a clear distinction between the two tiers of workers.

Growth of Independent Consultants and Contract Workers

Hiring independent consultants or outside contractors offers employers another way to reduce the size of the permanent payroll and lower benefit costs. Millions of Americans work for contract companies, and another million are classified as self-employed consultants—some by design, others because they have no choice. Simply by filing a form with the Internal Revenue Service and giving the worker a copy, an employer can transform a worker into a "self-employed independent contractor" and avoid social security taxes, unemployment insurance, workers' compensation, and laws regulating wages, hours, health and safety, and equal employment opportunity.

Migrant farm workers, clericals who work at home at computer terminals and many other kinds of workers have become self-employed contractors. The practice goes on even though employers have abused the IRS provisions and illegally classified workers as independent contractors. Of all available jobs in 1986, 9.3 percent were filled by contract employees—up from 5 percent in 1983. The proportion is expected to rise to 15 percent by 1990.[14]

Contract work has overtaken entire industries. Janitors, for example, used to work directly for a business or building owner; now most are employed by cleaning contractors. Almost 4 million people work for building services firms, guarding, cleaning, and performing other jobs that were once handled in- house. Almost 1 out of every 10 nursing shifts was filled by a temporary agency nurse in 1986.[15]

To the extent that contract employment blurs the employer-employee relationship, workers' rights are in danger. Often, an employer will hire a contractor or consultant in an attempt to circumvent job standards negotiated in a union contract. But the same employer will continue to have a strong hand in setting the terms of employment. In effect, many employees now have joint employers—a building owner *and* a cleaning contractor, a hospital *and* a temporary nursing agency, or an insurance company *and* a temporary clerical service. So slippery are the roles of the two parties that more than one group of unionized contract workers has been forced to go to court to protect their wages and job security.

For example, in 1986, Mellon Bank of Pittsburgh, Pa., terminated its cleaning contract with a unionized cleaning company and rehired the same 80 janitors as employees of a nonunion contractor. Overnight, full-time jobs were converted to part-time jobs without health or pension benefits. Pay dropped from $225 a week to as low as $38 per week. The janitors, members of SEIU Local 29, went on strike and filed suit in federal court, alleging that the bank was a joint employer and was bound by the original contract it had signed. In May, 1987, the National Labor Relations Board (NLRB) ruled that Mellon was indeed a joint employer and had violated federal labor law by unilaterally changing the terms of employment. Mellon agreed to pay over $850,000 in back wages and to restore the janitors to full-time status.

Another case involved protecting migrant farm workers against abuse of the independent contractor label.[16] Several Midwestern pickle growers had classified their migrant farm workers as independent contractors, claiming that the migrants were, in effect, self-employed workers with full control over the hours and conditions of their work—similar to high-priced consultants. The workers, however, were in fact migrants— working less than 140 days, earning only $4,000 a year on average, and living in poverty. Many were illiterate, unable to file their own tax and Social Security forms. In December 1987, a district court ruled that the workers were employees, with all the rights guaranteed under state and federal labor laws. The case is on appeal.

And in 1982, California Western States Life Insurance Company offered its insurance claims processors the opportunity to become independent contractors, enabling them to work at home rather than in the office. But although they were paid by the piece, without benefits, they were required to sign an agreement promising to work for no other company. The company raised quotas repeatedly until the workers were putting in 12 or more hours a day. On 1 December 1985, eight of the women quit their jobs and filed suit, charging that the insurance company had violated the California state labor code by classifying them as independent contractors simply to lower their pay and benefits. Although the California Employment Development Department ruled that the women were company employees, the case was settled out of court in May 1988.[17]

Privatization of Public Employees

In a parallel process, many government agencies, faced with federal funding cutbacks and lower tax revenues, are contracting out more and more jobs, such as garbage collection and food services, to private firms that promise to do the job for less. The federal government wrote $42 billion in nondefense contracts in 1987; state governments wrote $81 billion in private contracts in 1982—a threefold increase in less than a decade; and city and county governments wrote about $1 billion in contracts in 1986.[18] Privatization may seem like a foolproof way to cut costs and streamline operations. But the reality is not so rosy.

Private contractors cut costs largely by paying low wages and benefits. In effect, privatization is a way to eliminate middle-income public jobs and to create low-wage contingent work. Women and minorities who have found more opportunity in the public than in the private sector are particularly hard hit by the trend.

But when outside firms operate with lower wage scales, quality often drops. When Santa Clara County, Calif., turned prison food services over to a private contractor, prisoners went on a hunger strike to protest the deterioration in meal quality.[19] Many contractors lack the expertise needed to perform the service or save costs. Some deliberately bid low and then jack up prices once they have a lock on the service. Thus, when employees at Fort Bliss, Texas, and the Groton Naval Submarine Base Hospital in Connecticut took a closer look at some attractive bids they had received, they discovered that the bidders had omitted the costs of security, training, monitoring, and equipment maintenance.[20] And when the Department of Defense let nine contracts for cleaning, maintaining, and servicing equipment, the contractors overran their original bids by $73 million. By doing the jobs in-house, the department could have saved over $67 million.[21] Widely publicized incidents of waste and fraud by DOD contractors (the $640 toilet is the best-known example) should lend public officials a healthy skepticism toward privatization.

The Hidden Costs of the Contingent Work Force

As already noted, the growth of the contingent work force poses problems for individual employers as well as for the U.S. economy as a whole. Productivity, quality of service, attendance, innovation, and morale are all threatened when the tie between employer and employee is stretched to the breaking point. A 16-city survey, for example, found that most word processing supervisors were dissatisfied with the work performed by temporary employees. The Home Insurance Company reported that 70 percent of word processing temporaries do not work out.[22] And hospital and nursing home administrators have begun to fear for quality and continuity of care when the use of agency nurses means the staff changes every day.[23] As a result, the trend now is to try to hire temporaries for longer periods. After all, why should marginal employees go the extra mile when they reap few rewards from the process?

Businesses with a stable work force are 20 percent more productive than those without one.[24] It takes time and resources to orient new employees to perform even the simplest tasks. L.L. Bean, Inc, a mail-order company, finds it takes a full week to train temporary clerks to handle the six-week Christmas rush. Federal Express Corporation hired consultants to put new computer systems in place—and regretted it. According to a report in the *Wall Street Journal*, "the contracting process turned out to be highly inefficient." The consultants spent weeks mastering the firm's existing system and left without training most permanent employees how to use the new one. Federal Express plans to keep future projects in-house.[25]

Turnover and absenteeism are also problems for employers who turn full-time jobs into part-time ones. Many cleaning contractors who hire low-paid janitors experience such high turnover rates that they have trouble meeting their contract obligations. But fair treatment for part-time and contract workers pays off. Unionized cleaning contractors who offer good wages, benefits, and 40-hour weeks enjoy a much more stable and dependable work force. Equitable pay and benefits for part-timers can increase the quality of work, and lead to higher productivity, morale, reduced absenteeism and turnover.

Further, a growing body of research reveals that improved efficiency and quality of products and services is impossible without an ongoing exchange of information between managers and workers, as well as continual retraining. Transient workers are not around long enough to pass on many ideas to managers. Nor is there much incentive for employers to invest in training a worker who will be out the door tomorrow.

The growth of the contingent work force has taken a serious toll on the morale of permanent employees. The *Wall Street Journal* reports that many managers of large companies fear they will soon find themselves employed as "independent consultants" doing the same work for less money. So low is their morale, says the *Journal*, that they have "come to see their employers as the enemy."[26] As the president of a management consulting firm notes, "employee commitment is declining more than it ever has in the last decade."[27]

Solutions

Policies are needed to provide equity and job security for contingent workers, to stem the growth of the contingent work force, and to promote healthy flexibility in the workplace. And when a large percentage of the work force consists of part-time, temporary, and contract workers, a health and welfare system based on employer-paid benefits is clearly inadequate. "If we make the labor market flexible, but don't make the social welfare system flexible," notes Richard Belous of The Conference Board, "there are going to be lots of people falling through the cracks."[28] Public-private partnerships that provide all workers with health insurance, pensions, family and medical leave, and necessary job training are essential in today's work world.

Legislative Actions—Equal Pay for Equal Work:

Parity for part-time and temporary workers. Employers need to create part-time and temporary positions that not only can lead to full-time and permanent positions but also pay prorated wages and benefits. This would eliminate the economic incentive to turn full-time, permanent work into contingent work, and it would also relieve the burden on taxpayers who provide public assistance to low-wage workers without benefits.

—*Mandate prorated benefits for part-time and temporary workers by amending the federal Employment Retirement Insurance Security Act (ERISA) or the Fair Labor Standards Act.* Congress should amend ERISA [or FLSA] to require equal hourly compensation for part-time and temporary workers compared to full-time work. At a minimum, Congress should allow states the option of requiring benefits for part-time and temporary work. In Canada, federal and provincial legislation is pending that would require employers to provide prorated fringe benefits to part-time employees if those benefits are provided to full-time employees.

—*Cover part-time and "long-term temporary" workers in any minimum wage or benefit legislation.* Part-time and temporary employees who work a minimum number of hours or weeks should be included in any legislative proposals to expand health coverage or family and medical leave, and state and regional pooling mechanisms should help provide cost-effective benefits to these workers.

—*Reduce the number of hours required for pension vesting and improve pension portability.* Such actions would expand retirement coverage to part-time and temporary workers and ensure that contingent employees do not lose their pension benefits when they change employers.

—*Reform labor law to strengthen bargaining rights for part-time and "long-term temporary" workers.* Such bargaining units are much more likely to win prorated wages and benefits for part-timers—and to protect the jobs of full-time, permanent employees.

In spring 1988, the Minnesota legislature decided to study the use of part-time and temporary work in state service. Minnesota 9to5 is calling for study recommendations to include limiting the use of temporary workers only to situations that are truly temporary in nature, such as filling in for vacations/leaves or handling special projects.

Stem the growth of the contingent work force. Policymakers can take several steps to expand the number of full-time and permanent jobs.

—*Require public employers to convert long-term temporary into permanent jobs.* Public employers and contractors should be required to hire temporary workers on the permanent payroll after a specified period of time. States that already have such legislation on the books should enforce it. At the insistence of SEIU Local 790, the city of San Francisco agreed to convert 4,500 long-term temporaries (those with more than six months' seniority) into permanent employees. In addition, the federal government should repeal the 1982 Office of Personnel Management ruling that extends federal temporary worker status from one to four years.

—*Shorten the work week.* The standard work week in the United States is 40 hours: 1,900 hours per year with a 2½ week vacation. European countries have shortened the work week and lengthened the standard vacation. A shorter work week, without reduced pay, would provide full-time jobs to more people.

—*Enforce independent contractor laws.* Protect clericals who work at home and other independent contractors from violations of wage and benefit standards, step up inspections of home work sites, and prosecute violators.

—*Curb abuse of independent contractor status.* Wisconsin, Minnesota, and Colorado have acted aggressively to protect migrant farm workers and others against unfair treatment. The 1977 Wisconsin Migrant Act regulates many aspects of the employer-employee relationship, requiring minimum hours of employment, workers' compensation, and unemployment insurance. An executive order issued by the governor of Colorado requires prosecution of employers who intentionally abuse the independent contractor label.

—*Enact state and federal joint employer legislation.* Joint employer legislation ensures that firms that hire contractors are held legally accountable—along with the contractors themselves—for violations of fair labor practices. Such legislation was introduced in Pennsylvania in 1988.

Pass and/or strengthen federal and state legislation to protect existing union contracts when facilities change ownership.

—*Reduce and regulate privatization of public services.* Contractors should be required to meet or exceed wage and benefit scales paid to public employees doing similar work. Oregon and California impose such requirements on all state contractors. The federal Davis-Bacon and Service Contract Act require construction and service contractors to pay prevailing wages.

—*Provide public employees with the opportunity to compete.* In Oregon, before a public service is contracted out to a private company, the public employees union (SEIU Local 503) has the right to submit an alternate proposal. If it meets or beats the contractor's bid, the union's proposal must be accepted.

Establish open bidding procedures. Contractors should be required to disclose full details of exactly what they propose to do and how much they will charge.

Require all contracts to be paid on a fixed-cost rather than a cost-plus arrangement.

Enforce civil service laws that prohibit privatization of public services. (Courts have interpreted civil service laws in this way in some states, such as Ohio and Washington.)

Promote flexible mainstream jobs.

—*Expand temporary compensation programs.* Twelve states encourage employers to reduce work hours temporarily instead of laying off workers. The unemployment insurance system pays the difference in salary to those whose hours are reduced. Other states should adopt such programs, and the federal government should increase funds to support them.

—*Expand the supply of quality, affordable child and dependent care programs.* Women often work at home, at part-time jobs, or on night shifts at low pay with no benefits. They work irregular hours not by choice; rather, they lack affordable child care options. A national child care policy to expand child and dependent care programs would provide working women with real choices regarding their labor market participation.

Workplace Actions

Employers can take steps to achieve flexibility with equity on their own.

Provide equity and flexibility for part-time workers.

—*Voluntary reduced work schedules.* These allow employees to reduce their work hours with prorated pay and prorated (or full) benefits. Santa Clara County, Calif., has had such a program for its employees, members of SEIU Local 715, since 1979. The county also guarantees full benefits to employees whose hours are reduced involuntarily.

—*Permanent part-time positions.* One way employers can create part-time positions with prorated pay and benefits for employees who want them is through job sharing. Wisconsin has established a minimal quota for part-time civil service jobs that carry full seniority rights.

Convert temporary to permanent positions. There are many ways to meet changing demand without relying on temporary employees. Travelers Insurance Company retains a pool of retired employees who come to work on an on-call basis. Federal Express maintains a permanent pool of floating employees who are assigned to different departments as workloads change.

Career mobility. Employers should create career ladders for part-time workers and include part-timers and temporaries in job training programs and affirmative action programs.

Case Studies

In 1988, legislators in 15 states introduced a variety of bills to expand health coverage to part-time workers. Below are two examples from previous years.

Parity for Part-Timers in Wisconsin

State legislator Dismas Becker represents a district in Milwaukee, Wis., that has lost 85,000 manufacturing jobs since 1980. "These were jobs that provided good fringe benefits," he says. "Now the displaced workers are getting part-time jobs in the service industrics —jobs that pay close to minimum wage with no benefits."

At the urging of 9to5, Becker decided to introduce legislation to guarantee parity in pay and benefits for part-time and temporary workers. He soon learned, however, that ERISA will not allow states to require private employers to provide health benefits without a federal exemption. He redrafted his legislation to cover only state workers—"limited-term employees" who work fewer than 1,044 hours per year. (Currently, these employees can spend a lifetime working for the state without health benefits, pensions, or seniority rights.)

Under the proposed legislation, temporary and part-time state employees would be eligible for vacations, sick leave, holiday pay, and seniority rights on a prorated basis. The state would pay half the cost of health insurance and pension coverage for part-time and temporary employees who work at least 600 hours.

Health Benefits for Part-Timers in New Hampshire

Deborah Arnesen put in 40 hours a week at two small social service agencies. She had no health coverage. When she became pregnant with her first child, she had to pay several thousand dollars of medical bills out of her own pocket. Both of Arnesen's employers would have been happy to provide her with benefits, but they couldn't. Their insurance company, Blue Cross/Blue Shield of New Hampshire, did not allow part-timers working less than 30 hours per week in group plans.

In 1984, Arnesen was elected to the state legislature. She made access to health coverage for part-timers a priority. She proposed legislation to prohibit all insurance companies doing business in the state from excluding part-timers (those who work more than 15 hours a week) from group insurance plans. The bill became law in 1987.

By mandating coverage by insurers—not employers—Arnesen's bill sidesteps the limitations of ERISA, which bars states from requiring employers to provide benefits. Now that insurers cannot exclude part-timers, Arnesen is determined to make sure employers include them. She has proposed legislation requiring employers who provide benefits to full-time employees to offer their part-time employees the opportunity to participate in the group benefit plans.

Many of us have cleaned this building for 15, 25 and 30 years. These were good jobs that paid a living wage and benefits. Then our wages were reduced to the point where now I take home only about $100. And our health insurance and pensions were eliminated. . . . My daughter Kim has asthma and a heart murmur. I can't afford the doctor's visits and tests she needs. . . . Last month, the doctors told me I need surgery for a uterine condition. The public clinic won't perform the operation because I don't have insurance.

—Nina Pettiford, janitor, Pittsburgh, Pa.

Today, companies like ours pay for health care twice—once for our own employees, and then again, via taxes and inflated health insurance premiums, for the employees of those businesses who don't provide benefits for their own people. . . . I fear that we may be seeing the beginning of an unhappy trend by which employers will avoid providing health care benefits as a means of obtaining cost advantages over their competitors. It has already happened in the airline industry.

—Robert Crandall, chairman and president,
American Airlines

Thirty-seven million men, women, and children in this country have no health insurance coverage. Each year, one million more Americans join the ranks of the uninsured. Three-fourths of the uninsured are full-time workers and their families. As a nation, we now spend $425 billion a year on health care, and still the number of people without basic health coverage is growing. Since 1938, employers have been required to pay a minimum wage. It is time that we insist upon a minimum health care package for every working man and woman in our society. By so doing, we will help America's competitive position in the world.

—Edward Kennedy, U.S. senator, Massachusetts

Chapter 4:
The Erosion
of Employee Benefits

The passage of Social Security legislation in 1938 seemed to signal that the United States was on the road toward adopting a broad national program of social insurance.

It didn't happen.

Fifty years after Social Security, we are still far from the comprehensive public insurance programs adopted by every other industrialized nation save South Africa. Instead, we have a network of private insurance provided voluntarily by employers and supplemented by public programs for the elderly, the disabled, and the poor.

Before the 1930s few health insurance plans existed; Americans paid their medical bills themselves. During the Great Depression, hospitals faced with declining occupancy offered hospitalization plans, and from this Blue Cross was born.

Today's system took shape in response to wage controls imposed during World War II. Although employers could not increase wages, they found that by offering generous benefits—paid vacations and holidays, health insurance, and pensions—they could attract and motivate scarce employees. These benefits took hold first in the highly unionized manufacturing sector and soon spread through the work force as a whole. Then, in the 1960s, labor unions pressed for benefits beyond hospital care: fully paid health insurance (known as "first dollar" coverage plans), medical coverage for retirees, and pension plans to provide retirement security.

Through tax incentives, the federal government encouraged the growth of private sector programs. Federal tax deductions for employer-sponsored health insurance reached $3.3 billion by 1975; another $5.5 billion in subsidies went for pensions and individual retirement plans.[1] The government also carved out a modest direct role. In 1965, Medicare and Medicaid were enacted, establishing for the first time a federal responsibility to provide health coverage to nonworking elderly and poor Americans. Nine years later, Congress passed the Employee Retirement Income Security Act (ERISA) to establish minimum standards for eligibility and funding to protect workers' private pensions.

Despite this patchwork approach, our nation managed to make steady progress toward universal access to health care and retirement security. By the late 1970s, almost 90 percent of Americans had at least nominal health coverage. In addition, more than 90 percent of senior citizens received Social Security benefits, and half received an employer-paid pension as well.

Paying fringe benefits helped employers not just because the benefits were tax deductible but also because they reduced turnover and thereby boosted productivity. The social equation was working.

In the late 1970s, however, decades of progress toward universal coverage came to a halt, and a dramatic decline set in. Since 1980 the ranks of insured Americans have fallen from over 85 percent of the nonelderly population to 82.5 percent in 1986 (table 4.1),[2] at which time 37 million Americans—nearly one-fifth of the nonelderly population and nearly 8.4 million more than in 1980—lacked basic health coverage. And the ranks of civilian workers covered by retirement plans have declined by 4 million— from 56 percent of the total work force in 1979 to only 50.3 percent in 1983.[3]

Table 4.1:
Percent of Nonelderly Population with Health Coverage, by Sources, 1979-86

	1979	1983	1984	1985	1986
Employment-based	67.4	64.6	64.0	64.3	64.8
Other plans (including Medicare, Medicaid, Champus, and individual health insurance	17.9	18.5	18.3	18.1	17.7
Total Insured	85.3	83.1	82.3	82.4	82.5

Source: Table prepared by the CRS based on data from the March 1980, March 1984, March 1985, March 1986, and March 1987 Current Population Survey.

What happened? Business cycles, the transition to a service economy—these are only part of the answer. The basic reason for the decline of health coverage and retirement security is that American corporations opted out of the implicit "social contract" they had embraced for three decades. Pressured by world competition, they chose to sever their commitments to long-term workers and make products go for "cheaper," not better. Employers have thus swelled the ranks of part-time and temporary workers and independent contractors who lack fringe benefits, and they've allowed reduced benefit standards to spill over into the permanent, full-time work force, as well. Even the economic recovery of the 1980s hasn't put an end to the cutbacks. For many employers, health insurance and pensions are out of the picture for good.

The "no-strings work force" philosophy may increase short-term corporate profits, but only at great cost to the economy. While health coverage has declined, federal tax subsidies to employers nonetheless have ballooned to an estimated $25 billion in 1988, with $21 billion more in support to public hospitals and medical relief programs. Health care spending is expected to triple by the year 2000 to 15 percent of the gross national product.[4]

The erosion of workplace insurance has taken a human toll as well as an economic one. We spend 2.2 times as much per capita for health care as the average for the other Western industrialized countries. Yet our infant mortality rates are now as much as 1.7 times higher. Babies born in the United States have less chance of reaching their first birthday than do babies in 19 other countries.[5]

As for retirement programs, Social Security provides a bulwark against the kind of coverage crisis currently afflicting health care. But while today's retirees can depend on employer-sponsored pensions to supplement their Social Security checks, a growing portion of today's work force won't be so fortunate. Employers in 1988 are less likely to offer a pension plan at all. And today's workers change jobs frequently—63 percent of the growth of the work force during the last decade can be attributed to women, whose family responsibilities force them to have significantly lower job tenure than men—which thereby reduces the value of their pension.

Substantial reforms are necessary to relieve the strains on our health care and retirement systems. In our view, the only way to provide universal access to affordable health care is through a national health insurance program. In the meantime, however, public-private initiatives can go a long way toward providing both health and retirement coverage for all Americans.

The Decline in U.S. Health Care Coverage

As already noted, over 37 million Americans had no health coverage in 1986 (figure 4.1). (Thanks to Medicare's near universal coverage, only 300,000 of these were seniors.) Certainly some explanation lies with population growth: even if the *proportion* of Americans with health coverage had remained steady in the 1980s, the growing population alone would leave 2.4 million more people uninsured. Cutbacks in public programs are also partly to blame. But the biggest threat to universal health care has been the breakdown of health coverage in the workplace.

Figure 4.1:
Rapid Growth of Uninsured Americans in the 1980s

Millions of People

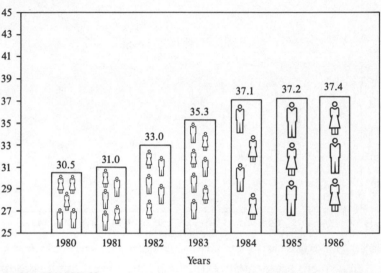

Years

Source: CPS, 1981-87.

We have seen how world competition has provided the impetus for corporations to cut back on benefit standards—including health insurance—for long-term employees. Skyrocketing health premiums haven't helped, either, but were in fact a catalyst for business's decision to break the social contract. In the 1980s, health care expenditures rose at a faster rate relative to GNP than ever (figure 4.2); today, health premiums are jumping 20-30 percent a year. These cost pressures stem from the diffusion of new technology and unnecessary medical procedures and tests. A recent RAND study confirms that 10-25 percent of hospital admissions are unnecessary.[6]

And employers have responded mainly by shifting their costs to workers, forcing them to pay more out-of-pocket. "First dollar"

Figure 4.2:
U.S. Real GNP Compared with
National Health Expenditures

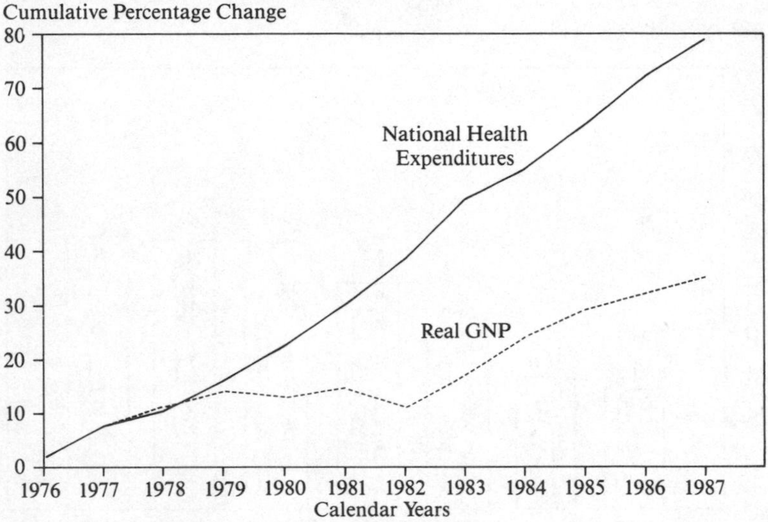

Cumulative Percentage Change

Calendar Years

Source: Division of National Cost Estimates, Health Care Financing Administration.

coverage plans are virtually extinct, and the cost of family group premiums has increased 66 percent in real terms over the last decade, worsening a growing family coverage crisis.

Nor has the government stepped in to lend a hand. Between 1981 and 1988, Medicaid, the major federal program providing medical care for poor families with children and long-term care for the indigent elderly, was cut by over 8 percent in real dollars; it now covers only 38 percent of those below the poverty line—down from 65 percent a decade earlier. And the Medicare program for the elderly has become a major deficit target, with cutbacks totaling $43 billion since 1981. But these are fake savings as costs have shifted onto the backs of our seniors, who now pay 34 percent more out-of-pocket (in constant dollars) for medical care.

Unfortunately, the decline of employer-paid insurance inflates health care costs throughout the system. Without such coverage, many of the working poor go without health care altogether. Others are forced to rely on public programs designed to serve only the nonworking poor and elderly. But those programs are already underfunded, ill-equipped to add working families to their clientele. Thus, many workers find themselves entering the public health system by the back door, receiving free care in a hospital emergency room. And such a system of hospital-based subsidized care is enormously expensive and inefficient.[7] Emergency room care costs far more than timely treatment in a doctor's office. To cover the cost of treating the uninsured, hospitals raise their rates to private pay patients by at least 10 percent,[8] so insurance premiums go up. Thus, companies that do provide adequate health insurance are forced to pick up the tab for those that don't, and when premium costs go through the roof, even those companies that provide begin looking for ways to shift costs onto workers or taxpayers. A vicious cycle of declining coverage takes hold.

If workplace health coverage had not fallen during the 1980s, there would be 5.5 million fewer uninsured people today and no U.S. health coverage crisis. (Declining workplace health coverage accounts for over 90 percent of the 6 million newly uninsured workers not explained by population growth.) Instead, *75 percent* of uninsured Americans in 1986 are workers or their dependents— two-thirds of them in families with full-time workers. Their employers don't pay for coverage, and they can't afford to buy it on their own.

And the future looks even more bleak since uninsured workers are overwhelmingly members of the new work force.

—*Most uninsured workers (65 percent) are employed in service industries*—retail trade, business services, entertainment and recreation, and personal and related services.[9] Two-thirds or more of workers in these industries have no health coverage on the job (figure 4.3),[10] and these industries are among the fastest growing in the nation, projected to account for 44 percent of the 21 million new jobs to be created by the year 2000.

—*More than two-thirds of workers (excluding the self-employed) without health benefits work in small businesses* (no more than

100 employees), and of these, 53 percent work in firms with fewer than 25 employees. At the other end, nearly one-quarter work for employers with more than 500 personnel, and 18 percent are in businesses that employ 1,000 or more.[11]

— *Uninsured workers are low-wage workers:* three-quarters of them earn less than $10,000 per year, and almost all (93 percent) earn less than $20,000.[12] About one-third of full-time workers who earn under $10,000 a year lack health insurance.

— *Uninsured workers are contingent workers:* part-timers, temporaries, and independent contractors. Fewer than one-quarter of part-time workers have health insurance from their employer; only 12 percent of those working less than 20 hours a week in large firms do.[13] About a quarter of temporary workers received workplace health coverage in 1987,[14] compared with three-fourths of the full-time work force.

Figure 4.3:
Workers Not Covered by Employer-Paid Health Insurance, 1986

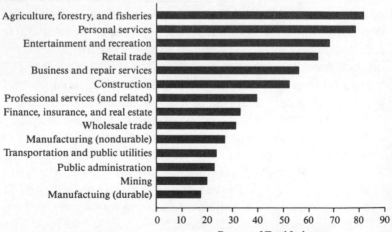

Source: CRS, March 1987 CPS.

Many workers have no health insurance because their employers don't offer it. In other cases, employers do offer health coverage but require workers to pay a prohibitive share of the costs. The massive cost shifting from employers to workers in response to spiraling health care costs—the major health care trend in the 1980s—has increased workers' out-of-pocket health care expenses by a shocking 66 percent between 1980 and 1985. Thus, many workers who enroll in health plans postpone necessary medical treatment for themselves or their families because they can't afford the up-front costs,[15] as was found to be the case by the SEIU in a 1987 survey among workers earning $10,000 a year or less.[16] And as a 1986 survey in Washington State confirmed, other workers can't afford to take the plan at all.

The employment-based health system has broad penetration because it covers workers, family members of workers ("dependent" coverage), and some retirees. Roughly half of all workplace coverage is for dependents. But the soaring cost of family premiums, which has increased 66 percent in real dollars over the past 10 years, has encouraged employers to sharply increase workers' share of the costs for family coverage or to drop it altogether. Thus, 69 percent of employees covered by group health plans had to pay for family coverage in 1986, compared with 62 percent in 1985 and only 50 percent in 1981, and these families paid an average 37 percent of the costs for family coverage.[17] Further, 93 percent of plans in 1987 had deductibles of $100 or more *per enrollee*, compared with only 65 percent in 1978.[18]

Given these trends, it is not surprising that the greatest decline in workplace coverage has been among spouses and children under 18 (figure 4.4). This worsens the growing family health crisis. Nearly seven out of eight uninsured children in 1986 lived in families with one or more working parents; more than half lived in families headed by full-time workers.[19] Employers are similarly looking to dump retiree health coverage (which covers 9.1 million retirees today) altogether or to force workers to pay the bulk of the premiums.

Figure 4.4:
Employment-based Family Health Insurance, 1979 and 1986

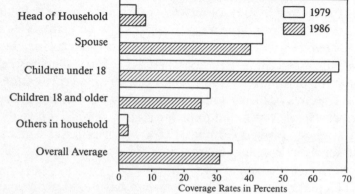

Source: CRS, March 1980 and 1987 CPS.

A 12-state survey of low-wage workers conducted by SEIU in 1987 illustrates how these costs actually add up. The survey found that although three-fifths of the workers were offered employer-based coverage, 52 percent didn't have health coverage. Some had no health plan at all, while others simply couldn't afford their plan's high premiums, copayments, and deductibles.[20] Among workers surveyed, family premiums averaged $130 a month, or 30 percent of take-home pay.[21] After that, workers faced family deductibles averaging $500 a year—equal to an entire month's pretax salary—and 20 percent copayments after that on covered services. It is not surprising, then, that half of the insured workers with children could not afford to cover them. (Nationally, one-fifth of all uninsured children live with a parent who has employer-sponsored coverage.) Many of these workers do without preventive care and turn to emergency rooms and public hospitals when someone gets sick. And *over 42 percent* of the uninsured workers surveyed by SEIU in 1987 said they could not afford to seek medical care or had been turned away by health providers. As previously noted, such a system endangers the health of the family and costs society plenty in excessive medical bills.

The Costly Lack of Health Coverage

The failure of employers to provide health insurance endangers the health of millions of workers and their families. A 1986 Health Interview Survey conducted by the Department of Health and Human Services showed that the uninsured population used only 64 percent as many physician services as the insured.[22] Almost 16 percent of uninsured pregnant women had not received prenatal care during the first trimester of pregnancy. A large survey conducted by the Robert Wood Johnson Foundation found a 65 percent jump in the numbers of Americans with no source of regular health care between 1982 and 1986.[23]

Although the health of the American population in general has improved since 1982, among uninsured Americans all health indicators have worsened. In 1985 alone, neonatal mortality rates increased by 3 percent among blacks and by 1 percent among all nonwhite infants. The incidence of babies with low birth weight in 1985 jumped back to the 1980 level (the first such increase since 1961). Of Americans with a serious illness such as cancer, heart disease, or diabetes, 17 percent did not see a doctor in 1986. Clearly, poor health care results in or perpetuates poor health.

Some pregnant working women and their children are eligible to receive food from the federal Program for Women, Infants, and Children (WIC). Programs such as this are cost-effective; it is estimated that every $1 invested in WIC saves $3 in reduced health costs.[24] But in 1985, WIC reached fewer than half of all children and women in need.

Other workers may be eligible for the Medicaid program if they meet the categorical tests (e.g., if they live in single head-of-household families). Few workers, however, have even this safety net.

Instead, those in need are forced to patch together health care through expensive hospital emergency rooms and outpatient services, thereby entering the public health system by the back door. As we have seen, it is an approach that is inefficient, costly, and unhealthy.

The Decline of Pension Coverage

The U.S. retirement system has been described as a stool with three legs: Social Security, pensions, and personal savings. Traditionally, it has taken all three legs to provide economic security after retirement. Indeed, half of today's retirees rely on pensions to supplement Social Security and savings.

(There are two basic types of pension plans: a defined benefit plan promises a fixed benefit determined by the plan design; a defined contribution plan—individual accounts, profit sharing, thrift plans—requires a fixed employer contribution but promises no fixed benefit. Only defined benefit plans have excess assets (plan assets in excess of the accrued benefits earned by all plan participants at the time of termination) to recover. In 1985, defined contribution plans were the basic pension for about 30 percent of covered workers; 70 percent were in defined benefit plans. About 40 percent had both types of plans.)

Pension coverage grew rapidly in the 1960s and 1970s. (Workers are said to be "covered" if their employer sponsors a pension plan.) By 1979, private pensions covered 56 percent of the total work force—up from 22 percent in 1950. But the 1980s have sharply reversed that trend (table 4.2). Despite the economic recovery, job-based pension plans had dropped to 52 percent of the total work force by 1983 and to an estimated 48.6 percent by 1985. Among private sector workers, pension coverage rates show a sharper trend, falling from 55 percent in 1979 to 50.3 percent in 1983.[25]

Because pensions are a source of investment funds, many employers have terminated pensions to recover money to use for other purposes.[26] Since 1980, they have terminated more than 1,600 pension plans for a total loss of $17 billion in retirement funds. In so doing, they have effectively taken back contributions they have made over the years to employee pension funds. Employees have virtually no say in how the reverted funds are used, and the terminated pension plan often is not replaced by another plan.

Table 4.2
Employment, Pension Coverage, and
Future Benefit Entitlement—1979 and 1983

	Employment (in thousands)		Pension Coverage Rate (percent)		Future Benefit Entitlement (percent)	
	1979	1983	1979	1983	1979	1983
Civilian employment (All employees and self-employed)	95,372	98,964	56.0	52.1	23.7	24.4
Nonagricultural wage and salary workers	85,181	88,214	61.1	56.2	25.1	25.2
Private sector employees	69,381	72,465	55.1	50.3	20.5	20.3
Government employees	15,800	15,748	87.4	83.0	45.3	47.4

*1985 estimates from the Employee Benefits Research Institute (EBRI) show a further decline in pension coverage to 48.6 percent of the civilian work force.

Source: EBRI and Department of Health and Human Services *CPS*, May 1983, and Department of Labor/Social Security Administration *CPS*, May 1979.

Many of the same workers who are without health insurance aren't covered by pension plans, either (figure 4.5, table 4.3).

—*They are service workers.* Only 22 percent of service workers are covered by pension plans, compared with 57 percent of manufacturing workers.[27] Among retail workers, only 19 percent are covered; of personal service workers, only 10 percent.

—*They work in small businesses.* In businesses with under 100 employees, fewer than 25 percent of workers are covered by pension plans. At companies with more than 500 workers, 82 percent are covered.[28]

—*They earn low wages.* Only 32 percent of workers earning below $10,000 are covered by pension plans, compared with 82 percent of those earning $25,000 or more.[29]

—*They are contingent workers.* Employers who provide pensions are not required to cover employees working fewer than 1,000 hours per year; only about one in four among such part-time employees is covered by a pension plan.[30] As for temporaries, when the Bureau of Labor Statistics first surveyed their pay and benefits, it didn't even bother to collect data on pensions.

Figure 4.5: Employees Covered by Pension Plans, Public and Private, 1985

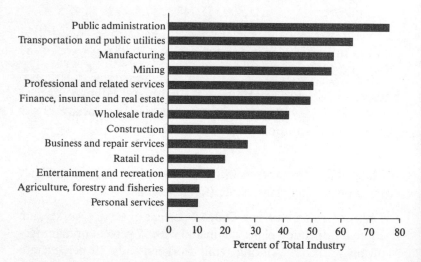

Source: Bureau of the Census, *Current Population Reports.* 1987

Table 4.3: Pension Coverage Among Nonagricultural Wage and Salary Workers, 1983

	Percent of Employed With Pension Coverage
Firm size—private	
Less than 100	22.9
100 to 499	58.1
500 or more	81.5
Job tenure	
Less than 1 year	29.4
1 to 9 years	56.2
10 and over	79.6
Hours	
Less than 1,000	27.5
1,000 to 1,999	50.5
2,000 and more	64.5
Earnings	
Less than $10,000	32.3
$10,000-$24,999	67.7
$25,000 and over	82.1

Source: EBRI/Department of Health and Human Services, *Current Population Survey*, May 1983.

But even among workers who are covered by pension plans, many will never collect a penny. In 1983, although 56.2 percent of non-agricultural workers were covered, only 25.2 percent were actually entitled to future benefits. Why? Like part-timers, some workers are ineligible to join up. And eligible workers earn the right to collect a pension (i.e., they "become vested") only after a certain number of years at a particular workplace. The Tax Reform Act of 1986 lowered the vesting period to a maximum of 5 years, down from the previous standard of 10 years. Yet, because the average job tenure for civilian workers is only 4.3 years,[31] many workers will still never qualify.

Women face special difficulties. Because many work part-time in service industries, they are less likely to be covered; and where covered, they are less likely to vest. (Average job tenure is 3.6 years for women, 5.0 years for men.) A 9to5 report on older workers notes that although 42 percent of working women participate in pension plans, only 20 percent—compared with 43 percent of men— receive pension benefits at retirement.[32] And when they do qualify for pensions, their benefits are paltry. As most women earn less than $15,000, their average pension earnings totaled only $370 per month in 1984 (men averaged $670). Combined with Social Security, women's retirement income was $740 a month in 1984 ($1,030 for men).[33]

Job mobility causes many to lose pension earnings entirely; others see their future pensions devalued. That's because the issued pension checks are typically based on years of service with the employer and on salary at the time of retirement or when the employee leaves. Thus, workers who vest here and there lose. So do the 20 percent of workers in their early forties with 15 to 20 years' tenure who will leave their job within the next 10 years.[34] Workers who change jobs lose an average 25 percent in pension earnings.[35]

Similarly, when an employer terminates a defined benefit pension plan, workers see their benefits eroded (i.e., valued at today's service credits and salary). How much they are eroded depends on whether the employer sets up a new pension plan and what type it is. Most observers note that when the new plan is identical to the old one (i.e., another defined benefit plan), beneficiaries lose little because past service credit is usually granted. But in 1987, employers in nearly two-thirds of terminated plans created either a savings account plan (i.e., a defined contribution plan) or no new plan at all. An American Association of Retired Persons study found that in such cases, beneficiaries are indeed losers: 50-95 percent or more of their expected benefit at retirement can be wiped out.[36]

What this all adds up to is that today's trends—a more mobile work force, the growth of a contingent work force, declining pension coverage, terminations of healthy plans—are jeopardizing tomorrow's retirement security for the baby boom generation.

Solutions

The current benefits system is not working. The implicit social contract that once guaranteed health coverage and retirement security to working Americans is collapsing. And the erosion of employment-based benefits has been accompanied by draconian cutbacks in public programs. But change is in the air. A growing consensus is building among business, labor, and government leaders that new public policies are needed both to solve today's health care crisis and to avert tomorrow's pension crisis.

Health Access: Legislative Actions

A national health care program is the only way to ensure that all Americans have access to affordable, quality care. Only such a program can enforce uniform standards of care. And only a single financing mechanism can effectively control the spiraling costs of health care. But until the emergence of a more favorable political climate for such a major undertaking, a package of intermediate, achievable reforms can move our nation steadily toward that ultimate goal. Such a package should include the following provisions:

Mandate employers to provide minimum health coverage to workers and their dependents or face tax surcharges earmarked for a state insurance fund. A federal mandate would reach nearly three-fourths of the uninsured, rebuild our faltering system of private health coverage, and spread the cost of care more equitably among firms. It would also conserve scarce public health dollars that now go to subsidize those employers who do not provide health coverage. Any mandate should seek broad coverage for part-timers and temporary workers who are currently excluded from most health plans.

Expand Medicaid to supplement employer-paid coverage so that no worker will be forced to forgo participation in a private plan because of prohibitive costs, and reform Medicaid to better serve the nonworking population. Use the Catastrophic Insurance Bill of 1988, which includes a Medicaid "wrap around" provision to help relieve the elderly of the burden of high premiums and copayments, as a model for the working poor with private insurance. Reform Medicaid by removing categorical restrictions, setting uniform eligibility standards of at least 100 percent of poverty, and improving provider participation and reimbursement rates.

A healthy start on life should be the right of all children born in the United States. By expanding Medicaid to cover uninsured pregnant women and young children with income up to twice the poverty level, we would help make this right a reality.

Create public and privately funded insurance pools to guarantee coverage to the disabled and unemployed. Currently, the seven state risk pools in operation (eight more are in the works) are for those who can afford to buy insurance but are unable to do so because previous medical conditions exclude them from private plans. These risk pools are expensive, serve a total of only 20,000 people, and require heavy public subsidies. But larger-scale pools financed by public and private funds, like the one established in the Massachusetts Health Security Law of 1988, could serve all those who cannot get insurance through the workplace or public programs.

Provide tax incentives to encourage employers to prefund retiree health coverage as they now do for pensions. Retirees are not eligible for Medicare until age 65. Rapid health care inflation, more early retirees, and the downsizing of work forces in the 1980s point out the need to prefund retiree health benefits rather than continue funding them on a "pay as you go" basis. (Estimates of total unfunded liabilities range from $100 billion up to $2 trillion.) Unless these and other steps are taken now to protect retiree health benefits, the number of uninsured in this segment of the population will increase.

Make it easier for small businesses to afford health insurance through pooling mechanisms, phase-ins, and tax incentives. Over half of all uninsured workers work for businesses with fewer than 25 employees. The biggest barrier to these businesses offering health insurance is the heavy administrative fees, which can be 20-30 percent more for small businesses.[37] Pooling mechanisms can reduce such costs substantially. Other steps to reduce the burden for small businesses include phase-ins of employer mandates and tax incentives; the latter includes achieving parity with corporations by allowing self-employed individuals, partnerships, and other unincorporated firms to deduct 100 percent of their health premium costs, rather than the 25 percent currently allowed these groups.

Establish a new financing system for long-term care that covers both nursing home and home care benefits. Currently, the Medicaid system is too overburdened to bear the high costs of nursing home care and also serve the poor. A new financing mechanism for long-term care should remove nursing home payments from the Medicaid program. Coverage for home health services should be expanded to allow our nation's elderly to live in dignity.

National reforms that forge a public-private partnership represent an opportunity to build on past progress toward the goal of ensuring that virtually all Americans have access to affordable, quality health care. Currently, a significant expansion in public insurance *alone* would displace employer-paid coverage and add considerably to the federal budget deficit. Similarly, without Medicaid reform, employer mandates *alone* would also be problematic; unless deductibles and copayments are picked up by wrap-around insurance, mandated minimum health benefits will result in high cost sharing for low-wage workers. Further, some part-timers who work few hours and those working for very small businesses are likely to fall through the cracks as the legislation is shaped by political compromise. A cooperative effort can build on both bases to ensure that no one is left out of the system.

Until such national reforms are enacted, states have an important role to play. The Massachusetts "universal coverage" program is a good model to follow.

Health Access: Workplace Actions

Employers can take steps to improve access to health care on their own.

Create multi-employer and managed care programs to make health insurance affordable to small businesses. In Tulsa, Okla., for example, a coalition of over 20 large employers created the Tulsa Health Option Plan, administered by the Chamber of Commerce, which offers Health Maintenance Organization (HMO) and Preferred Preference Options (PPO) coverage to small firms. In the first nine months of operation, 11,500 workers enrolled.

Such programs can work for municipalities as well. In the San Francisco Bay area, several small local governments have joined together to form a large health plan pool, with built-in cost containment features, that offers benefits at low prices to public employees. Premium costs have dropped 20 percent since the arrangement began.

Initiate managed care programs to make health insurance affordable to workers. Low-wage employees of the multimillion-dollar Beverly Nursing Home chain in Michigan could not afford the high deductibles and premiums required by the company's health plan. Their union, SEIU Local 79, negotiated with the chain to make less expensive options available. The 1987 contract initiated an HMO arrangement that is cost-effective and affordable.

Ensure benefit parity to improve access to health care for part-timers and temporary workers. A recent survey showed that 68 percent of the firms exclude part-time employment from health coverage; half exclude employees who are seasonal and temporary.[38] Employers should create part-time and temporary positions that pay prorated wages and benefits.

Pension Access: Legislative Actions

The erosion in pension coverage presents no immediate crisis for today's retirees. But we must act today to protect those who will retire tomorrow by (1) expanding pension coverage and (2) ensuring adequate retirement benefits.

Broaden coverage to include part-time and temporary workers. Currently, close to 40 percent of all part-time workers are employed for fewer than 1,000 hours a year (about 20 hours a week).[39] The Employment Retirement Income Security Act (ERISA) of 1974, the federal pension law, allows pension plans to exempt these employees and to impose a one-year waiting period for eligibility. ERISA should be reformed either to mandate prorated benefits for temps and part-timers or to shorten the waiting period and require coverage for those who work at least 500 hours a year.

Liberalize vesting standards for workers. Currently, vesting standards mean that only about 30 percent of plan participants are entitled to future retirement benefits. The five-year vesting standard mandated by the Tax Reform Act of 1986 added about 1.9 million more vested workers.[40] Lowering vesting standards further to three years would extend coverage to more workers and would especially benefit women.

Protect workers' benefits when plans are terminated. Employers seeking to recover excess assets by terminating healthy pension plans should be required to meet higher thresholds before they can take out the money and should pay penalties at rates that discourage withdrawals. Plans should cushion benefits to protect against losses in the event of market downturns like the October 1987 stock market crash. And employers should be required to share excess assets among active and retired workers. In addition, employers should be given financial incentives to establish defined benefit replacement plans so as to minimize benefit losses to workers.

Make pensions more portable. Social Security is a portable pension system: benefits accrue for all jobs in one pot over your entire career. A universal and uniform pension system that covered all employers and accommodated job mobility would be tantamount to an additional Social Security tier. Examples of such a comprehensive system include the mandatory contribution tier recommended by the 1980 President's Commission on Pension Policy, and the French system, in which defined benefit plans are organized around occupations.

Short of such a system, two alternative proposals could be pursued. First, defined benefit plans could be required to do more for short-term workers through an arrangement known as a "floor offset," under which an employer sets up an individual account (a defined contribution plan) for workers as well. All workers would receive *either* the pension, promised by the defined benefit plan, *or* the annuity financed by their defined contribution plan, whichever was higher. Workers with short tenures would receive more from defined contribution annuities. Workers changing jobs would get the most favorable benefit option to them. Second, mechanisms could be developed that enable workers to roll over vested benefits into a pension vehicle, perhaps a federal bank where vested pensions would be deposited when a worker leaves his or her job.

Provide more incentives to encourage pension plan formation. Policies are needed to increase coverage by smaller employers. Proposals include a mandatory uniform system; tax credits that cover start-up costs for small businesses; and voluntary measures, including the establishment of portable pension plans by pension asset managers.

Alternatively, Congress could make simplified employee pension plans (SEPs) a requirement for those employers who do not sponsor a qualified retirement plan. SEPs are like individual retirement accounts (IRAs) and were designed with small businesses in mind: they greatly streamline the paperwork and other administrative burdens.

Extend the scope of ERISA to public pension funds. Currently, there are no minimum pension standards protecting workers in state and local governments. New federal standards should be tailored to recognize the unique issues affecting state and local governments.

Case Studies

Los Angeles County Home Care Workers

Los Angeles County employs 40,000 workers to care for elderly and disabled people in their homes. These home care workers earn only $3.72 per hour and have no health insurance. In 1988, SEIU conducted a survey to find out how they obtain medical care for themselves and who pays for it.[41]

About 7 percent of the home care workers are covered by direct public insurance—that is, Medi-Cal or, for those age 65 or older, Medicare. But over 60 percent have no health insurance coverage from any source, and 54 percent of those uninsured workers turn to publicly funded emergency rooms or county hospitals while the other 9 percent use community clinics as their primary source of health care. (In sharp contrast, of those Los Angeles County workers who have private health insurance, 60 percent use doctors offices for their routine care.)

The taxpayers' bill for public health care for Los Angeles County's home care work force totaled an estimated $21.4 million in 1988, of which $8.3 million came from hospital emergency room and outpatient care.

A basic employment-based health benefits package for these workers would conserve substantial public health funds, already in short supply. The public would save hospital indigent costs paid through both higher taxes and the higher premiums that companies pay to insure their workers. Private and county hospitals in California are at present shouldering more than $1 billion in uncompensated care. Additionally there would be savings to the public health insurance system, as the workplace health plan would become the first payor of health claims and the public plan (e.g., Medi-Cal) would become the secondary payor, responsible only for those benefits not covered by the private plan.

If this one employer had provided basic workplace health insurance, the public would have saved $15.1 million in 1988. By 1992, the annual savings would be $28 million a year.

And these estimates understate the likely savings to California's public health system. Private health insurance would greatly improve access for these and other low-income working women to cost-effective prenatal care and other early medical treatment.

Massachusetts' Health Security Care Act of 1988

In 1988 the Massachusetts legislature adopted the Universal Health Security Act of 1988 that will provide coverage to an estimated 600,000 uninsured state residents by 1992. The program requires public and private employers to provide coverage to employees or pay tax surcharges.

Coverage must be provided to full-time employees (over 30 hours per week) who have been employed for at least three months, and to part-timers (at least 20 hours per week) who have been employed for at least six months or who are the head of a household.

Employers who do not provide coverage will contribute to a state pool. For employees earning less than $14,000, the employer's contribution will be 12 percent of wages. For those earning $14,000 and above, the contribution will be $1,680. Employers must also pay a 0.12 percent surcharge on their unemployment insurance contributions to cover unemployed persons without health coverage.

Exempted from these provisions are firms that employ five employees or fewer, and firms that have been in operation for less than three years. Seasonal workers are also exempt.

A pool will be created to buy insurance for employees of small businesses, and a program will be established to assist small businesses for which the required contributions exceed 5 percent of gross revenue.

State of Washington's Basic Health Plan

In 1987, Washington state adopted a trial insurance plan that will offer health coverage to about 30,000 uninsured residents in five regions of the state. The law subsidizes a basic health plan that will be offered to all. Families earning under twice the federal poverty level are eligible.

Participants will pay monthly premiums on a sliding scale basis. Those below the poverty line will pay about 10-15 percent of the premium costs; those at the upper end will pay the full cost of the premium. A high risk pool covers individuals with preexisting conditions. The program is financed by the general fund and fees, not by payroll taxes as in Massachusetts.

Wisconsin Program Provides Health Care to 9,000 Uninsured

In 1984, the Wisconsin state legislature initiated the Wisconcare program, providing free outpatient care, prescription drugs, laboratory tests, and maternity care to the uninsured. Eligible families must earn below 150 percent of the poverty level, and participants must not be employed for more than 25 hours per week. The program costs the state $3 million a year and is funded by assessments on hospitals. In its first two years, Wisconcare operated in 17 counties with high unemployment rates and served 9,000 people—2 percent of the state's 450,000 uninsured residents.

In 1986, a state commission recommended six pilot programs to test ways to build on the initial successes of Wisconcare:

—Health insurance vouchers for workers whose employers do not provide benefits.
—Subsidies to help insured workers who cannot afford the premium costs.
—A Medicaid buy-in plan for the disabled and those with serious health conditions.
—Funding to help small businesses establish health plans.
—A loan program for the temporarily uninsured.
—Expansion of Wisconcare.

Although the state legislature approved all six programs, which would have cost $350 million, the governor vetoed all except two: the Medicaid buy-in pilot and the small business program. The

Robert Wood Johnson Foundation has funded the Health Choice Small Business Program, which is designed to improve access to health care for self-employed people and small businesses.

National Health Insurance in Canada

For a successful model of national health insurance, we need look no further than Canada, where a universal system delivers cost-efficient, high quality care. The origins of the Canadian system can be traced to the years after World War II, when several provinces, starting with Saskatchewan, set up hospital insurance programs. In 1957, the federal government enacted the Hospital Insurance and Diagnostic Services Act and picked up half the tab. And in 1965, it offered financial support to the provinces to establish universal insurance for physician services.

Except for long-term care, nonprescription drugs, and adult dental care, Canadians have access to a full range of publicly funded services. Consumers have a free choice of providers, and the programs carry a low price tag compared with medical care in the United States.

Health care expenditures totaled 8.6 percent of Canada's gross national product in 1985, compared with 10.7 percent in the United States. This can be partly explained by Canada's low administrative costs, which in 1986 averaged only 1.3 percent of Canadian health expenditures, compared with 5 percent in the United States.

Canada also faces a health inflation problem although the gap is not as wide as it is in the United States. Nonetheless, Canada remains steadfast in its commitment to universal health coverage. Efforts to address financial pressures today seek to balance protection of patients with the need to invest increased funds in plants and equipment. A commitment to access as well as cost constraint has been crucial for achieving both goals.

We have a lot to learn from our Canadian neighbors.

America has become a society in which everyone is expected to work, including women with young children.... The institutions and policies that govern the workplace should be reformed to allow women to participate fully in the economy and to insure that men and women have the time and resources needed to invest in their children.

—William B. Johnston,
Workforce 2000: Work and Workers in the 21st Century

My son was hospitalized three times for epileptic seizures. My husband and I alternated taking time off from work to be with him in the hospital. I missed only six nights of work in seven months. But my supervisor and personnel manager said that if I missed one more night of work in the next six months, they would fire me or ask me to resign.

—Tina Hurst, former packer for a large
pharmaceutical company, Newark, Del.

I'm up at 6 A.M., getting the kids dressed and fed. Then I take Bryce to the babysitter. Bianca and I take two buses and the subway to her day-care center. I hop in a cab to be at work by 9 A.M. During school vacations, my daughter Shana, who's 11, watches Bianca. I've got it pretty well juggled— unless I miss a bus or have to work overtime, or one of the children gets sick. The trouble is, I'm exhausted all the time.

—Alexandria Perry, secretary, Washington, D.C.

Chapter 5:
Work and Family

The decades of the '70s and '80s put the American family under enormous pressure. Lower wages cut into buying power so severely that the average middle-class family came to need two incomes just to stay even with yesterday's standard of living (figure 5.1). In 1987, an urban family of four needed $19,400 to survive on a no-frills budget, yet most individual workers earned less than $12,500. If women had not flooded into the work force, family income would have plummeted a full 18 percent between 1973 and 1986.[1]

A rise in single-parent families also forced many mothers into the work force. And expectations of women changed. Most women came to assume they would spend a lifetime in the labor force—either because they had to work, or because they liked to work, or both. The result of all these factors is that between 1973 and 1988, American families sent nearly three quarters of all available adults into the work force.

Nor have mothers of young children been exempt from this mass movement into the work force. In 1960, only 19 percent of women with children under age six were in the paid work force. Today, 57 percent are, including even most mothers of infants.[2] And given the severe labor shortages predicted for the coming decades. The U.S. economy will continue to need women workers. By the year 2000, demographers predict, 75 percent of young children will have working mothers (figure 5.2).[3]

Figure 5.1: Annual Income Compared to Bureau of Labor Statistics Low-Income Budget

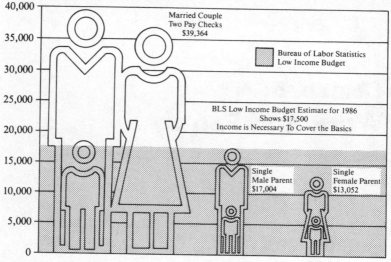

Median Annual Income in the U.S.

Married Couple
Two Pay Checks
$39,364

Bureau of Labor Statistics
Low Income Budget

BLS Low Income Budget Estimate for 1986
Shows $17,500
Income is Necessary To Cover the Basics

Single
Male Parent
$17,004

Single
Female Parent
$13,052

Figure 5.2: Growth of Working Mothers, 1960-87

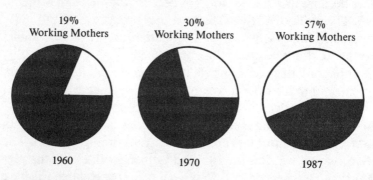

19%
Working Mothers

30%
Working Mothers

57%
Working Mothers

1960

1970

1987

Source: Bureau of the Census

Changes in work patterns have brought changes within the family itself. Some of these changes have been beneficial: the stereotype of a generation ago, with its commuter dad and home-bound mom, is gone for good (figure 5.3); men's and women's roles have become more fluid; many women have greater opportunities; and some men have assumed more home responsibilities. But problems have also emerged. With far fewer women at home, there are serious gaps in care for children, the elderly, and other dependents. Too often, there is no choice but to leave children or elderly relatives in an environment that provides poor supervision and little stimulation and inadequate care.

Productivity at work suffers as well. Many overstressed working parents and caretakers have no choice but to come in late, take days off, work less efficiently as they worry about day care arrangements, or leave their jobs with little notice when emergencies arise.

Figure 5.3:
Family Employment and Earnings Characteristics

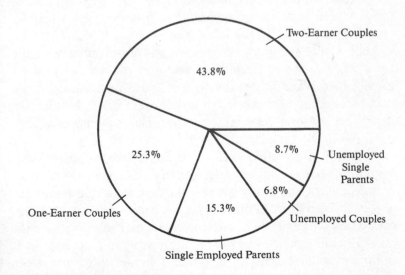

Source: BLS, *Employment and Earnings*, 4/88

Balancing the Demands of Family and Workplace

Thus, working women and men with dependent family members shoulder a heavy burden with few supports from employers or public programs. As the Economic Policy Council of the United Nations Association of the United States noted in its 1985 landmark report, *Work and Family in the United States: A Policy Initiative:* "Our national interest will best be served if we can enable working parents to concentrate on their jobs without neglecting their families. We can no longer leave to chance an area of policy so primary to our country's social and economic fabric."[4] Both private and public programs are needed to help working people balance their dual roles as workers and as family members.

Family Leave Policies

When hospital technician Robin McCabe of Seattle, Wash., was pregnant with her second child, she requested 11 weeks of maternity leave. Her leave was approved by her supervisors, but when she reported back to work, her job was gone.

James Callor's six-year-old daughter was in and out of hospitals for a year as she was treated for cancer of the nervous system. Finally, there was no more the doctors could do. Callor took his daughter home and requested time off from work to be with her during her last few weeks. His employer, a large mining company in Helper, Utah, turned him down.

When employers refuse to allow workers to take temporary leave from work upon the birth or adoption of a child or a serious illness of a dependent, too many women and men must quit their jobs altogether, even when all they need is a few days, weeks, or months off. No worker should be forced to make such a choice. With a little bit of flexibility, employers can retain valuable employees at little or no cost, and workers can keep their jobs and reduce the stress of balancing home and work responsibilities.

Eighty-five percent of working women have a baby at some point during their careers. Almost half go back to work within months of giving birth. But because of rigid employer policies, many cannot return to the jobs they were in before giving birth.

Or perhaps an employer is only willing to grant a few weeks off for the period when the new mother is disabled by childbirth; many women (and babies), however, need a longer period of adjustment. (The American Academy of Pediatrics recommends a minimum of six months of parental leave to help new mothers and babies adjust.) Because her employer will not allow her to take a few months off, the new mother may have to quit her job and pound the pavement looking for a new one. During this period, taxpayers may foot the bill for her medical costs, food stamps, and other expenses. Still another woman might give in to her employer's demands and return to her job when her baby is still tiny. Neither the family nor the employer comes out ahead under such a system.

The United States is one of only two industrial nations (the other being South Africa) without a national parental or maternity leave policy (table 5.1, next page). Such policies, which allow new mothers, and sometimes new fathers, to take time off to care for a newborn, have been adopted by 135 other countries, including many in the developing world.

—In Europe, five to six months of *paid* leave is the norm for new mothers.

—Even in Japan, where labor standards often lag behind those of Europe, new mothers are guaranteed 12-14 weeks of paid maternity leave.

—In Canada, new mothers receive 15 weeks of leave with 60 percent wage replacement.[5]

Why does the United States lag behind the rest of the world? In part, labor shortages have forced other nations to urge women into the work force by accommodating their needs. But, in addition, other societies recognize more fully that raising the next generation and caring for the elderly are vital tasks that require public investment and employer accommodation.

Table 5.1:
Parental and Maternity Leave Policies,
United States vs. Selected Countries

Country	Duration	Amount	Recipient
Canada	17-41 weeks	60%/15 weeks	mother
Italy	22-48 weeks	80%/22 weeks	mother
West Germany	52 weeks	100%/14-18 weeks	mother or father
Sweden	12-52 weeks	90%-38 weeks	mother or father
Austria	16-52 weeks	100%/20 weeks	mother
Chile	18 weeks	100%/18 weeks	mother
United States	0	0	0

Sources: International Labour Organization Global Survey, *Women at Work*, 1984; Sheila B. Kamerman, Alfred Kahn, and Paul Kingston, *Maternity Policies and Working Women* (New York: Columbia University Press, 1983).

In contrast, parental leave in the United States is a private affair. As of this writing, the only piece of federal legislation in this area is the 1978 Pregnancy Discrimination Act, requiring that *if* a company provides temporary disability coverage, it must treat pregnancy-related conditions like any other disability. But only about 40 percent of all working women have such coverage,[6] and only about half of all large companies (and many fewer small ones) allow mothers to stay out with their newborns for a few months beyond the period of disability. Even fewer allow any significant time off for fathers.[7]

Similarly, many workers face a temporary crisis when a parent, spouse, or child has a serious medical emergency. Only a handful of private employers allow employees to take time off under such circumstances; only a third allow employees to use sick days or personal leave to care for a sick child.[8] A 1980 Gallup poll found that worry about caring for ill children comes right after child care as the biggest concern of working parents.[9]

Family leave policies make sense in both the short and the long term.

—The absence of a national family leave policy *costs* American families and taxpayers an estimated $363 million every year in reduced earning power and public assistance programs for the unemployed and uninsured, according to economists Heidi Hartman and Roberta Spalter-Roth.[10]

—A mandated family leave policy would cost employers little, according to the government's General Accounting Office (GAO). Many firms would cope with the short-term absence of their employees in the same way they now deal with vacations—simply by shifting workloads or hiring relatively inexpensive temporary employees. By retaining experienced employees who would otherwise quit, employers would save on recruitment costs; their only new cost would be that of providing health insurance to employees on leave.[11]

—Most employers who do have a parental leave policy say it helps them recruit and retain workers.[12] And it helps them in one more way, as well: unions report that, in this era of concession bargaining, employers do not ask for givebacks on parental leave.[13]

These benefits have been borne out by experience. For example, more than half the work force at Home Box Office, Inc. (HBO) in New York City is female, with an average age of 32 years. Seeking to retain talented, experienced employees, the company offers a variety of policies, including flexible scheduling programs such as flex-time and part-time work with full benefits. Further, new mothers receive disability leave with full pay and benefits; fathers and adoptive parents receive 1 week of paid leave; and new parents are allowed 12 additional weeks of unpaid leave. To Shelly Fischel, HBO vice president for human resources, the benefits of these policies are readily apparent. "Many of the women who return to work after giving birth do *better* at their jobs than they did before."

Similarly, *Fortune* magazine gives Merck and Company, Inc., top marks for its "ability to attract, develop and keep talented people." One reason Merck has been able to do this is a wide range of programs that helps employees balance work and family life. These include a parental leave policy that provides 6 weeks of paid maternity leave followed by up to 18 months of unpaid child care leave with full medical benefits; a child care resource and referral service and on-site day care center; financial support for several nearby day-care centers; and flex-time provisions that allow employees to begin work anytime between 7:00 and 9:30 A.M. and leave eight hours later.

Flexible Work Schedules

The school day does not match the 9:00 to 5:00 work day. To meet their family obligations, many workers need flexible scheduling policies, such as flex-time (in which workers may vary their arrival and departure times, so long as they are at work during a "core" period in the middle of the day), part-time work *with* benefits, and job sharing (in which two part-time workers split one job).

New York State's Voluntary Reduced Work Schedule program, for instance, allows employees to work part-time without loss of benefits or job security. Negotiated with the Public Employee Federation, the program covers 54,000 professional, scientific, and technical workers in New York State. With the agreement of their supervisor, employees may choose to reduce their work schedules in 5 percent increments with prorated pay and full benefits. A variety of flexible scheduling options are permitted, including reducing daily work hours, taking certain days off each week, and taking off for an extended period, such as the summer. The program has helped retain valuable employees and avert layoffs in a time of public sector cutbacks.

Child Care

Workers have families all year around—not just at the annual picnic. That means family issues are business issues. Every working parent knows that good day care is too hard to find and very hard to pay for. 3 o'clock every day, people wonder where their kids are. Workers who are worried about whether their children are safe and well cared for can't possibly work at full potential. That makes child care a productivity issue.

No commercial facility is built without allowing room for employee's cars. It's time we had at least as many day-care slots for our kids as we have parking spaces for our cars.
—Barbara Mikulski, U.S. senator, Maryland

Most working parents have trouble finding good day care at prices they can afford.

Insufficient supply. A 1986 Harris poll found that almost a third of parents have difficulty finding the child care arrangements they want.[14] There are long waiting lists for subsidized child care slots. Seattle and New York City, for example, have space for only about one of five children who need child care. The shortage of infant care is particularly acute. In addition, several million children of working parents are unsupervised before and after school.[15] California alone has a shortage of 500,000 after-school child care slots.[16]

High costs. Lack of affordable day care is the prime problem facing low- and moderate-income families. Full-time care for preschoolers costs an average of $3,000 per child—almost half the annual income of a minimum-wage worker,[17] infant care may cost about one-third more. Child care consumes about 10 percent of an average family's household budget; among low-income families, however, it consumes roughly 23 percent, comparable to the amounts spent on food and housing.

Inadequate quality. There are no federal child care standards, and most states lack the resources to enforce their own licensing requirements. As a result, too many children spend their days in settings that are merely custodial or downright dangerous. Many children lack the continuity of care that is essential for their development. According to a recent University of California at Los Angeles study, children whose providers change frequently demonstrate less self-control and less confidence.[18] And annual turnover among providers in group programs averages 42 percent, second only to that among gas station attendants.

Despite the numbers—2 million infants, 10 million preschoolers, and 16 million school-age children with mothers in the paid labor force—too many employers and policymakers still see child care as a problem requiring individual rather than public solutions. The federal government spent less on child care at the end of the 1980s than it did at the beginning. No national child care legislation has been passed since President Nixon vetoed the Child Care Development Act in 1971, calling it "antifamily." The only national child care program that helps working parents today is the Dependent Care Tax Credit, which returned an average of $347 to each participating family in 1986. Ironically, low-income families—those who pay no taxes or who cannot afford the upfront costs of child care—receive no benefit from this program. And federal child care programs specifically designed to help poor families were severely reduced during the Reagan years. (For example, funding for Title XX of the Social Service Block Grant, which supports child care programs, was cut in half [adjusted for inflation]).

Meanwhile, only about 3,000 of the 6 million U.S. employers provide any kind of child care assistance.[19] Six hundred firms have workplace child care centers; another 825 provide some form of financial assistance; and about 1,600 firms offer either a resource and referral program or a flexible benefit plan that forces employees to choose between health insurance, pensions, or child care benefits.[20]

Many representatives of the business, labor, academic and policy making communities agree that investing in child care is of utmost importance for children, families, and the economy as a whole.

—A 1987 *Fortune* survey found that 70 percent of working mothers suffer stress and 41 percent report absenteeism due to family responsibilities. Good child care arrangements improve job performance and punctuality.[21]

—Of corporations that offer child care programs, 95 percent responding to a 1982 national survey reported measurable benefits in the workplace, including reduced absenteeism and tardiness, and increased productivity, performance, and morale (table 5.2).

—Low-income children enrolled in preschool programs like Head Start are more likely to graduate from high school and are less likely to commit crimes or become teen parents than those not in such programs.[22]

—Child care enables low income mothers to leave public assistance and enroll in job training programs. One in three non-working mothers would go to work if they could find affordable child care.[23] Every dollar invested in preschool education returns $4.75 in savings to society in lower welfare costs and greater worker productivity.[24]

Table 5.2: Employers Noting Workplace Benefits of Employer-Supported Child Care

	Percent
Morale	90
Public relations	85
Staff turnover	65
Absenteeism	53
Productivity	49
Tardiness	39

Source: Sandra L. Burud, Pamela R. Aschbacher, and Jacquelyn McCroskey, *Employer-Supported Child Care: Investing in Human Resources* (Boston, Mass.: Auburn House, 1984), p. 22-28.

Elder Care

The elderly are the fastest-growing group in the nation. Traditionally, most elderly men and women have been cared for by women relatives. Today, with most women in the work force, an expensive and heartrending crisis of care is upon us.

Keeping elderly dependents at home has benefits for older Americans and taxpayers alike. The alternatives are scarce and costly. In 1986, only about 24,000 adult day care center slots were available nationwide, costing an average of $150 a week. Home care services cost between $300 and $400 a week; few are covered by Medicare. And nursing home care costs about $22,000 a year, enough to deplete the savings of many middle-income Americans.

At least 2.2 million people provide care to elderly relatives outside of institutions. There may be more. A 1986 University of Bridgeport survey of several Connecticut-based companies found that between one-quarter and one-third of all employees over age 40 were caring for an elderly parent. At least a third of today's caregivers are in the labor force.[25]

Juggling caregiving and work responsibilities takes its toll on employees (table 5.3). At least 11 percent of caregivers eventually quit their jobs because the pressures are so great.[26] But many can't afford to quit, no matter how great the stress. About one-third of all caregivers are in the "sandwich" generation, still raising their own children while also caring for frail parents. And many of those responsible for elderly care must struggle to pay nursing homes, home health aides, or adult day-care centers.

Gaps in the Medicare program cause many families to become destitute when an elderly parent or spouse needs long-term medical care. Expanding Medicare to cover long-term care at home or in a nursing home would benefit workers and their elderly parents alike.

New workplace policies would also help. Many caregivers need temporary leave from work to help elderly parents recover and find new care arrangements in the wake of an illness like a heart attack or stroke. Others need flexible work schedules or reduced hours to help balance their family and work responsibilities. Only a handful of companies accommodate such needs.

Table 5.3: Work Arrangements Made by Caregivers to Accommodate Caregiving

Work Arrangements	Percent of Caregivers
Worked fewer hours	21.0
Rearranged schedule	29.4
Took time off without pay	18.6
Quit work	11.0

Source: R. Stone, G.L. Cafferata, and J. Sangl, "Caregivers of the Frail Elderly: A National Profile" *Gerontologist*, v. 27, N. 5 (1987) pp. 616-626.

SOLUTIONS

To meet the needs of today's working family, public policymakers must develop elder and child care programs and set workplace standards that accommodate these needs. Employers must also take action. Key areas for attention are (l) family leave, (2) flexible work schedules, (3) child care, and (4) elder care.

Family Leave: Legislative Actions

Pass federal and state legislation. Step one is to pass state and federal legislation requiring employers to provide a period of *unpaid* family leave upon the birth or adoption of a child or in case of a serious illness of a dependent.

By 1988, 5 states (Maine, Minnesota, Oregon, Rhode Island, and Wisconsin) had passed *parental* leave legislation, and 13 others had implemented *maternity* leave laws.

Step two is to join the rest of the industrial world and pass legislation that provides a period of *paid* leave so that new parents and caregivers can afford to take time off from work. Five states (California, Hawaii, New Jersey, New York, and Rhode Island)

and Puerto Rico have Temporary Disability Insurance (TDI) programs that provide benefits to new mothers.

Family Leave: Workplace Actions

Adopt family leave policies. Employers should provide six months to one year of leave with full health benefits to allow both men and women to care for a newborn, an adopted child, or a seriously ill family member. In addition, employers should make at least part of this period a *paid* leave.

Flexible Work Schedule Programs

Employers should initiate flexible scheduling programs such as the following:

—job sharing, in which two or more employees share the responsibilities of one job;

—flexible work schedules, whereby an individual's working hours may begin or end earlier or later than normal working hours so long as a core period is included;

—a voluntary reduced work schedule, whereby employees and employer mutually agree to reduce the number of work hours;

—policies that allow employees to use personal sick days when their children are ill. Some employers provide sites or funds for sick child care.

Flexible work schedules should provide prorated pay and benefits, job security, and career opportunities.

Child Care: Legislative Actions

Increase public support for child care. Many states and municipalities have experimented with programs to address the quality, supply, and affordability of child care programs. California, for example, provides approximately $315 million in direct funds for a wide variety of child care programs, while several of its cities have also developed unique approaches to *increase funding* for child care:

—A 1985 San Francisco ordinance requires downtown office building developers either to include child care space in new buildings or to contribute $1 per square foot to a child care fund.
—Fremont considered in 1988 a tax to finance prefabricated child care centers that will be attached to 30 elementary schools.

And nine states have supplemented their Head Start programs with state funds. To improve quality, Connecticut and Massachusetts have tied these funds to salary raises for day-care workers.

But while more state and local efforts are needed, only federal action can provide the resources to solve a national problem. Necessary components of federal child care legislation include the following:

—Measures to improve the *quality* of child care, including licensing standards, establishment of resource and referral agencies, and training and higher pay for child care providers.
—Initiatives to increase the *supply* of child care, including loan funds and tax credits to employers that support child care.
—Programs to increase the supply of school-based after-school care. Fees should be on a sliding scale with subsidies for poor children.
—Increased prekindergarten programs in the public schools. Twenty-two states have initiated school-based preschool programs for 3-to 5-year-olds.
—An expanded Head Start program to cover all eligible children. Today, only 20 percent are enrolled.
—Programs to increase and expand child care subsidies for low- and moderate-income working parents and for those enrolled in school or job training programs.
—Measures to improve the coordination of resources at the state and local levels.

While such measures would be important first steps, they only begin to address the needs of the 26 million children with working parents. Ultimately, our nation must develop a universal system of child care, just as we created our educational system 100 years ago. Until then, efforts to make child care more affordable will continue to clash with those to upgrade the quality of care. Child development experts, for example, uniformly agree that low salaries ($12,500 a year for full-time teachers and $10,000 for teacher aides) are the main barrier to improving quality of care. But in a recent study of the cost of care in four hypothetical day-care centers, higher salaries raised the price of child care by 37 percent; improving both salaries and staff-to-child ratios increased the cost by nearly 80 percent. Public financing would provide the resources to raise provider salaries, upgrade the profession, and take other actions to improve quality of care.

Child Care: Workplace Actions

Assistance with child care. While public programs are essential to help the working family, individual employers can also help workers meet their child care needs with

—construction of on-site child care centers;

—subsidies for child care expenses;

—pretax payroll deductions for child care expenses;

—resource and referral services; and

—financing of after-school and vacation child care programs at the workplace or in the community.

Some large employers (notably state governments in Massachusetts, California, and New York) have made child care funds available to individual worksites. Other companies have formed consortia to fund after-school programs, home day-care providers, sick child care, and community child care centers.

Elder Care: Legistlative Actions

Expand Medicare to include long-term home health and nursing home care. This would enable the frail elderly and other dependents to live in the community for as long as possible and would eliminate the need for workers to quit their jobs to care for them. It would also provide help to working families saddled with nursing home fees.

Elder Care: Workplace Actions

Assistance with elder care. Employers can provide resource and referral services; ensure that health insurance benefits cover home health care and nursing home care for dependents; and provide dependent care assistance plans or dependent care subsidies. Employers should also provide six months to one year of leave with full job guarantees and health benefits to allow both men and women to care for a seriously ill family member.

Case Studies: Family Leave

Temporary Disability Insurance and Parental Leave in Rhode Island

Rhode Island is the only state that has passed both a TDI program and a parental leave law.

The TDI program, established in 1942, is funded by a payroll deduction equal to 1 percent of a flexible wage base. Benefits equal 60 percent of an employee's average weekly wage over the previous two-year period. A woman experiencing a normal pregnancy and birth receives an average of 6-8 weeks of compensation; 10-12 weeks in the case of complications. The program is financially solvent. All private sector employees are covered, and according to an independent study by The Conference Board, workers do not abuse it.

The push for parental leave legislation began during Richard Licht's 1986 campaign for lieutenant governor. Licht "assembled a grassroots task force to learn about the issues of concern to working women," says chief of staff Maureen Maigret. "Out of this process came a policy paper supporting a state parental leave bill."

Although the business community opposed the idea, Maigret says they eventually "accepted the fact that the legislature in Rhode

Island is profamily and that this bill addresses the needs of the changing work force." Business organizations ended up joining in negotiations to refine the bill.

The resulting legislation, passed in 1987, provides support to fathers, adoptive parents, and new mothers wishing to delay their return to work beyond the period of disability. The bill provides 13 weeks of unpaid leave upon the birth, adoption, or serious illness of a child. Employers must continue health insurance coverage during the period of leave (employees prepay the benefit and are reimbursed upon their return to work). Businesses with 50 or fewer employees are exempt.

"It's a reasonable and sensible law," says Maigret. "We do not expect to see the economic chaos the business community claimed would result from parental leave legislation. In fact, we feel that the smaller employer will voluntarily adopt this policy just to be competitive with the large employer."

Family Leave in Wisconsin

In April 1988, Wisconsin became the first state to pass *family* leave legislation. The Wisconsin Family and Medical Leave Act includes two weeks unpaid leave to care for sick family members—children, spouse, or elderly dependents—in addition to six weeks unpaid leave for new parents. The law applies to firms with 50 or more employees.

A much stronger version of the bill, introduced by state senator John Plewa, passed the state Senate with a decisive and bipartisan majority in October. It would have allowed for up to 20 weeks and applied to more employees, but Republican governor Tommy Thompson vowed to veto anything more than 6 weeks maternity leave.

What changed the governor's mind was a delegation of children organized by Milwaukee 9to5. The children included 9-year-old Noah Michealson, who had cancer four years earlier; Jenny Weisenberg, also 9, whose asthmatic brother occasionally needed emergency treatment; and Craig Miller, age 7, who had been hospitalized briefly after being hit by a car. The children met with John Tries, secretary of employment relations, who admitted: "[We] tend to forget there are people involved and not just a concept. When the kids come to you, you remember what you're really talking about." The next day's headline announced, "Young lobbyists win lawmakers' hearts."

Governor Thompson agreed to add a provision for sick family members. At the bill signing April 26, he acknowledged the role of the children and for the first time conceded that the length of leave may need to be expanded.

Case Studies: Child Care

When Government, Union, and Employers Work Together: The Chinatown Child Care Center

In the early 1980s, many garment workers in New York's Chinatown had to bring their children to work, lock them up at home alone, leave them with neighborhood babysitters who were caring for as many as 10 infants, or take work home. Only a handful of child care centers served the community of 200,000 people. But even if there had been more centers, most Chinatown families couldn't have afforded their fees. Family income for two-paycheck families in the area averages only about $15,000 a year.

In 1982, a group of Chinese-American garment workers began to pressure for the construction of a new child care center that would provide subsidized care. They formed a committee, circulated petitions, conducted surveys, and sponsored fundraisers in support of the cause. And they approached their union, the International Ladies Garment Workers Union, as well as employers and the city government.

According to Katie Quan, one of the organizers, "the employers helped us. They knew this would help them in the long run. It would let the younger women, who are faster workers, come back to work. And it would reduce absenteeism and cut down on the illegal practice of bringing children into the shop."

Faced with funding cutbacks, the city child care agency was looking for partnerships with employers. Together, the union, garment workers, employers, and the city agency found a site and worked out a funding arrangement. The Chinatown Child Care Center, opened in 1983, today serves 80 children, ages 2½ to 6 years. Employers pay 40 percent of costs. The federal Job Training Partnership Act picks up about 55 percent of the tab. Parents pay the remainder, averaging about $10 a week.

Massachusetts Leads the Way in State Child Care Efforts

Massachusetts has a $130 million program aimed at improving the quantity, quality, and affordability of child care. The program has several components:

—*Resource and referral network*. Twelve agencies with 21 offices around the state train home day-care workers, provide technical assistance to day-care providers, develop community-based child care partnerships, and help parents find child care.

—*Subsidies*. Child care spaces for 18,000 children from low-and moderate-income families are subsidized. (The cutoff point is 115 percent of the state median income.) Also subsidized are 11,000 children whose parents are involved in the state's welfare-to-work program.

—*Corporate child care office*. Employers, unions, and employee groups receive technical assistance in setting up child care programs.

—*Revolving loan fund*. The fund provides financing for renovation and construction of child care centers. New England Telephone contributed $750,000 in matching funds.

—*Higher pay for child care workers*. Wages for workers in all centers that hold state contracts were raised by 49 percent to an average of $18,000 per year.

—*Child care for state employees*. Over 30 state facilities have on-site child care centers. A state labor-management committee has a budget of $225,000 targeted to improving child care programs for state workers.

Ten-year Grassroots Effort in Alabama
Wins Child Care Funding

When the federal government cut child care funds in 1981, the state of Alabama failed to make up the difference. As a result, its poor families saw the number of child care subsidies shrink by half—down from about 12,500 in 1981 to only 6,500 in 1987.

In response to the federal cuts, a statewide organization of child care providers, the Federation of Child Care Centers of Alabama, organized a coalition of over 100 state human services agencies to lobby for more funding. FOCAL had a series of successes.

In 1986, the group led a hard-hitting campaign to kill an administrative measure that would have dropped *all* child care funding from the state budget. One year later, thanks to FOCAL's efforts and those of other child care advocates, a special Joint Governor's-Legislative Task Force on Child Care was established; it recommended that subsidized child care become a permanent part of the state's budget.

"Elected officials no longer perceive child care subsidies as a welfare issue," says Jack Guillebeaux, deputy director of FOCAL. "Now child care is an economic development issue. It is widely understood that economic growth in this state depends on helping working women to join the work force."

By 1988, the state planning office had begun to incorporate child care as a part of its economic development strategy.

Money is still a problem, however. State funding for child care subsidies remains low—only about $10.9 million in 1987. "The state of Alabama has the lowest taxes in the nation," says Guillebeaux. "We now face a $100 million shortfall in the state budget. Unless we cut money from other essential social services, we simply can't afford more child care subsidies. The federal government must help poor states like ours to provide support for child care."

School-based Child Care in Seattle

A 1986 survey conducted for the city of Seattle, Wash., found 22,000 children needing child care and fewer than 9,000 slots available. The mayor's office turned to the public schools as "logical locations for child care programs," says Billie Young, the city's child care coordinator.

In 1986, voters overwhelmingly approved a $17 million bond levy that included funding for child care to be based in 14 new elementary schools. By fall 1988, 4 such centers had opened. The remaining 10 centers will open by 1992.

The centers are run by community-based providers selected through a competitive bidding process. The city's Commission for Children and Youth sponsored community meetings to determine the child care needs of parents in each neighborhood. One center is designed for children aged two months to five years. Three will include "latchkey" programs for school-age children, and several offer extended day care for children enrolled in Head Start and half-day kindergarten programs.

The school district levy funds pay for construction of the 14 centers as part of an ongoing capital construction program. Each program operator is responsible for generating operational costs from parent fees, grants, and other fundraising activities. Subsidies are available to low-income families. The city provides technical assistance to each new site during the start-up phrase, as well as ongoing training and monitoring for quality.

Examples from Abroad

Parental leave and child care programs in other countries demonstrate that a comprehensive national system is affordable—and works.

Parental Leave in Sweden

The Swedish Parental Insurance program, adopted in 1974, includes the following provisions:

—a childbirth allowance that allows new mothers or fathers up to 6 months off work at 90 percent pay.

—an extended care allowance that allows fathers or mothers to stay home with their infant for an additional 6 months, with 90 percent wage replacement for the first 90 days and a smaller amount for the second 90 days;

—a temporary care allowance that allows either parent up to 60 days of leave per year to care for sick children. A parent may also use the allowance to stay home when a day-care provider is ill.

The program is financed by employer contributions to a government insurance fund.

National Child Care Program in France

France has a public system of universal child care. Funding is provided by parent fees and by local and federal taxes.

Children of working parents under age two are cared for either in family day-care homes or in day-care centers. Local municipalities contribute the bulk of operational costs, with sliding-scale parent fees and national funds making up the remaining expenses.

Most children between the ages of two and six attend a free nursery school program, for which the state government pays most operational costs, with added funding from national and local governments. Teachers are supervised by the Ministry of Education.

As jobs change, as companies shut down and open up and move around, the only way a worker can survive and get promoted is to be flexible and to be able to change. If we don't prepare people for that, then we set them up to fail.

— Robert Jones, assistant secretary for employment and training, Department of Labor.

All of us licensed practical nurses [LPNs] have had this hanging over our heads. If LPN positions are abolished, I would have to start a whole new profession.

— Nancy Stambaugh, nurse from Plymouth, Mass.

I was laid off 17 days short of retirement. A few from the mill took their lives. Others lost cars, homes. Me, I just hung on. [When I went job hunting] people didn't come out and tell me, but I could tell they thought I was too old.

— Raymond Woolaghan, former steelworker from Homestead, Pa.

Sixty-five percent of the job applicants who come into our bank don't have the basic skills they need even to complete an application.

— James Howell, chief economist, Bank of Boston.

Chapter 6:
Employment and Training Policies

After almost two decades in a Pittsburgh steel mill, Raymond Woolaghan was not prepared to change careers. After the factory shut down, it was two years before he found a new job—a low-skilled position at half his former salary.

Nancy Stambaugh, a licensed practical nurse in Massachusetts, could have faced the same dilemma. A national trend toward eliminating LPN positions and replacing them with registered nurses threatened her job. But Stambaugh's union negotiated a groundbreaking program that allows her to prepare for a new career *before* her job becomes obsolete. In two years, she will graduate as a registered nurse.

Global competition and technological advances are changing the work world at a prodigious pace. The result could mean tremendous opportunity for workers. Elimination of dead-end jobs; reduction in routine, dull tasks; safer workplaces; and enhanced quality of life, including more leisure time, are all possible in our new service economy.

But it's not happening. Instead, millions of American workers are suffering from displacement and wage loss. Between 1981 and

1986, 1 in 10 American workers lost a job because a plant closed, a product market dried up, or a job was phased out.[1] Displaced workers often have trouble finding employment, and when they do, their new jobs frequently require fewer skills and pay less than the old.[2]

The mobility of capital and the rapid development of new technology require a flexible, highly skilled work force that can develop and implement new innovations and adapt quickly to changes in methods of production. In such an environment, investing in job training—especially in programs that continuously upgrade the skills of our workers—is essential, not only for the well-being of the work force, but also for the strength of the economy as a whole. Most U.S. companies, however, fail to invest significantly in developing their human resources. In 1982, for example, their spending on worker training averaged only $300 per worker, compared with $3,600 per worker spent on capital improvements.[3]

Individual employers have a variety of reasons for not spending much on training and worker education. Some are reluctant to provide training because they lose out on workers who do not stay around long enough to provide a return on the investment. Others, motivated solely by a short-term profit incentive, do not recognize the long-term benefits of a highly skilled, committed work force.

A public commitment to education and training is urgently needed to fill the gap left by private corporations. Implementation of a coordinated national training policy that pools the economy's resources for the benefit of all (workers and employers) would eliminate our current underinvestment in human capital. Individual employers would no longer have to bear the full cost of maintaining a skilled work force; at the same time, they would profit directly by society's commitment to invest in training and education.

Unfortunately, we lack a national approach. Currently, the United States falls far behind other nations in government spending on education and job training—a paltry 0.5 percent of the federal budget. In contrast Sweden spends 20 percent of its national budget on training, while France requires employers either to spend 1 percent of profits on training their own workers or to contribute to a national training fund. Even Singapore spends 6 percent of its gross national product on job training.[4]

In the past, it was our highly skilled and literate labor force that enabled the United States to maintain a relatively high-wage economy and lead the world in economic growth.[5] Today, broad application of new technologies has the potential to stimulate growth once again while also creating more challenging, interesting work. But that potential will be lost if we do not do a better job of training the work force.

A comparison of the automation process in two pulp mills studied by Harvard University business professor Shoshana Zuboff illustrates the importance of training if our nation is to reap the maximum benefit from the new technology. Managers of one mill invested $200 million in new equipment but allocated almost no money for worker retraining. Plant operatives who had once overseen production on the shop floor now sat in air-conditioned booths reading computer data about what was happening in the production areas. But with only minimal training in the new system, the workers couldn't make sense of the data and made little use of it. The return on the capital investment fell far short of expectations. At the other pulp mill, however, an innovative engineer convinced top management to teach a group of workers how to analyze and experiment with the computer data. As workers became actively engaged in improving the product, productivity and quality soared.[6]

The need for a national commitment to job training will only increase as more plants close, more job functions change, and the rate of growth in the labor force declines. We will not have new entrants to the labor force, fresh from college and schooled in the latest technology available to fill job openings in the future.[7] An older work force will have to be provided with the tools to meet the challenges and needs of the future. Without a coordinated training effort, we will risk creating a permanent underclass of the unemployed, the underskilled, the young, and the displaced, at the same time that skilled job openings go unfilled.

Investment in education and training must be accompanied by policies to achieve full employment, to stimulate job creation in regions with high unemployment, and to improve the quality of jobs. Public policies that invest in human capital are critical to our ability to improve productivity and compete in a global economy. Unless we make that investment, productivity in the service sector will continue to stagnate and U.S. standards of living will decline.

All of us will gain from public and private policies that develop rather than discard the talents of our most valuable resource: people.

Problems for New Entrants: Inadequate Public and Vocational School Training

Today, most workers must be able to read and write as well as solve problems and communicate effectively (figure 6.1). With the rapid changes in the economy, they must be lifelong learners. Yet as much as 20 percent of the current work force is functionally illiterate.[8] When the New York Telephone Company undertook a large-scale recruiting effort in 1987, it found that over 80 percent of applicants from New York City failed exams in basic reading and reasoning skills.[9] Not surprisingly, then, many workers can't get into the job market, and many companies have trouble finding qualified workers.

A sizable number of those who are currently working also lack the basic skills they need to advance. Motorola Corporation estimates it spends million a year teaching employees the basic skills they never learned in school.[10] And displaced workers have trouble gaining the job skills they need to advance or find new jobs. The United Auto Workers discovered that many displaced auto workers could not train for new careers without basic remedial education.[11]

U.S. public schools are responsible for most basic skills training. Numerous reports, however, have decried the poor quality of U.S.

public education, and in 1983, the National Commission on Education declared the United States "a nation at risk" because of the failure of its public schools. But the commission's recommendations—later echoed by many others—cost money. During the Reagan years, federal education expenditures declined 14.6 percent (adjusted for inflation), and the federal share of education funding dropped from 10 to 6 percent—down to its lowest level since 1964.[12] Many states and localities that have passed education reform packages lack the funds to implement them.[13]

Figure 6.1: Educational Requirements for Jobs of the Future (Table 18 from Solutions)

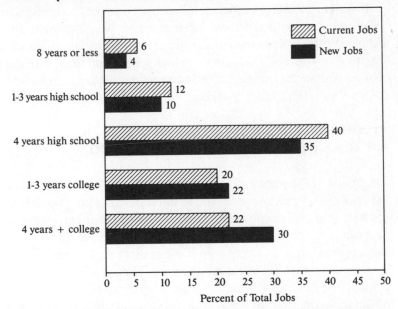

About half of the nation's high school graduates do not go on to college. Many depend on high school vocational education programs to prepare them for the work world. But these programs are underfunded and out-of-date: they lack modern equipment, and their teachers are often out of touch with current job requirements.

Moreover, there is little opportunity for on-the-job experience. More than half the students learn skills they never use—and never learn the ones they need.

Most students who are not college-bound are left to sink or swim as they enter the labor market. Few employers are eager to hire 16-or 18-year-olds into their first jobs.[14] Almost 1 in 10 young adults aged 16-25—and 1 in 3 black youths[15]—was without a job in 1988. The economic position of those without a college education has deteriorated in the 1980s as our manufacturing base shrunk. The pay gap between college- and non-college-educated young people widened to about 50 percent in the 1980s, compared to 15 percent in the 1960s and 1970s.[16]

There are examples of successful partnerships that integrate the public schools with the local labor market. Best known is the Boston compact, a program under which local businesses guarantee jobs to all youth who graduate from high school and work with the schools. But such business/school partnerships are rare and limited to areas with tight labor markets.

Inadequate Training Programs for the Low Skilled and Unemployed

Outside of the public schools, many programs have been put in place over the years to help move unemployed and low-skilled workers into decent jobs. The newest generation of employment programs, notably the Job Training Partnership Act (JTPA) of 1982, provides funds to local communities that create private industry councils controlled by local businesses. The PICs determine job demands and allocate grants to train workers to fill those jobs.

But the system is erratic and underfunded. It fails to provide adequate remedial education, specific skill training, or job counseling. Little or no attention is given to job *survival* skills training or to job retention efforts. In fact, with a median length of stay of 13 weeks there's no real training at all. Local employment and training programs mainly engage in job searches and so are most likely to serve those who are easiest to place in jobs and avoid those who are most in need.

Nor does the system come close to providing the supportive services—child care assistance, health benefits, and transportation stipends—that poor people need in order to participate.

Clearly there is a growing need for such programs, yet federal investments in job training declined dramatically during the Reagan years (table 6.1). In 1980, federal job training programs provided $10.8 billion to service 3.7 million men and women. By 1988, spending was down by $5.6 billion—a 65 percent cut in real dollars—and only half as many people were being served. Despite the emphasis on work programs for welfare recipients, the Work Incentive (WIN) program, which provides the funds, has been cut back by 82 percent in real terms. As a result, a 1986 congressional study concluded that of the millions of disadvantaged and displaced workers, it is likely that no more than 5 percent are being served.

Table 6.1: Unemployment Rate vs. Federal Funding Cuts for Job Training Programs

	Percent Unemployment Rate (April 1988)	Federal Job Training Program	Percent Funding Cuts 1981-88
Youth	15.6	Job Corps	4.0
Single mothers	8.4	Work Incentive program (WIN)	82.5
Blacks	12.4	General job train-	65.0
Hispanics	9.0	ing programs (JTPA)	
All workers	5.4		

Sources: BLS, *Employment and Earnings*, May 1988, and *Budget of the United States Government FY 1989* and *Historical Tables: Budget of the United States Government FY 1989*.

These cutbacks come despite evidence that training programs are cost-effective. A 1982 study by the National Council on Employment Policy found that every dollar invested in on-the-job training returned $2.28 in social benefits, including postprogram earning gains and welfare savings. The Job Corps program returned $1.39 per dollar invested.[17]

In recent years, several state governments have stepped into the gap left by underfunded federal job training programs, offering, in the words of a National Governors' Association report, "to share some of the responsibility of worker training with firms as a way of promoting the public interest in increasing productivity and competitiveness and preventing job loss."[18] A variety of state programs work in partnership with employers to prevent displacement, teach workers new skills, ease transitions for those who lose their jobs, and help move the long-term unemployed into the labor market. The most successful train workers for job openings at specific firms.[19]

Displacement and Waste: Consequences of a Failed System

One million men and women are displaced by plant closings, layoffs, and technological innovation each year. Unlike other industrial nations, the United States has few mechanisms to help these workers change jobs or plan for retirement. Employees in large firms receive an average of only one to two weeks' notice in advance of massive layoffs or plant closings.[20] A purchasing manager with 17 years' tenure at Dresser Industries, an international supplier of equipment and services in the natural resource field, received only five days' notice of a forced early retirement scheme. "Can you imagine what it's like when you're 63 years old and out of the clear blue sky, you're told you'll have to live on a week's pay every month?" he asks.[21]

In August 1988, after a protracted legislative battle, a plant closings bill was enacted into law, providing for 60 days notice to workers in businesses with 100 or more employees and the community prior to the closing of a plant. This law is a first step in easing the dislocation caused by plant shutdowns and unanticipated job loss. Its passage puts the United States on a par with other industrialized countries in this regard.

Early notification of layoffs or closings when coupled with counseling and job placement assistance has proven to increase the chances of reemployment.[22] The extra time also allows workers to develop better individual employment strategies and reduces the emotional stress on workers and their families. And it's cost-effective, as well. According to a recent Economic Policy Institute study, notification of at least eight weeks reduces future joblessness by almost four weeks.[23]

Yet early notification is only part of the solution. Recent studies find that people who lose their jobs, even with advance notice, still have difficulty finding new ones. Nearly 19 percent of prime age males who lost their jobs between 1979 and 1982 were still unemployed in January 1984.[24] Of those re-employed, 46 percent experienced earnings losses of 10 percent or more.[25]

Many dislocated workers are not in contracting industries. Too many U.S. companies choose to fire current employees and hire new ones when new technologies are introduced or when job functions shift for other reasons. Yet continual retraining makes good business sense. It boosts productivity, enhances a firm's ability to embark on new ventures, and builds commitment among employees. It also reduces the recruitment costs for employers and guarantees that the skills required are, in fact, available in an existing pool of employees.[26]

In 1988, every hospital experienced—almost daily—the effects of the nursing shortage. Hospital vacancy rates for registered nurses stood at 11.3 percent. A rational work force policy, one that incorporates training and career development, could help alleviate this shortage. Registered nurses who now leave the field because they lack career development opportunities or whose only avenue for advancement is in management, must be offered career development programs that allow them to deliver direct patient care.

Likewise, licensed practical nurses, who are being laid off as hospitals hire more registered nurses, need career ladder programs to become registered.

While the private sector spends billions on training and retraining, its efforts focus largely on management. (The private sector accounted for roughly half of all dollars spent on training in the 1980s.[27]) A recent Conference Board survey found that only 18 percent of manufacturing firms provide nonexempt workers with training programs, compared with 33 percent for managers. Another survey, conducted by the Bureau of National Affairs, found that 60 percent of the firms provide training to managers, 50 percent to professional and technical employees, and—again— only 18 percent to nonexempt employees. Small businesses, the catalyst of current job creation and innovation in the U.S. economy, provide the least training in both surveys.[28]

The federal government has not stepped in to fill this vacuum. To date, dislocated worker assistance programs have been limited to wage stipends (through the Trade Adjustment Assistance Program) and some demonstration worker assistance centers (funded through Title III of JTPA).[29] While these programs have made a difference, they are reactive, ad hoc in nature, and short-lived. Worse, they have largely ignored involving the private sector in shared retraining initiatives.

In the absence of a national program, efforts have been made at the state level and between individual employers and unions to fill the void. The California Employment Training Panel (ETP), for example, helps employers retrain current and laid-off workers. Created in 1983, the program has trained and placed more than 43,000 men and women. A 0.5 percent employer tax—paid into the state unemployment insurance system—raises about $55 million a year to fund the program. (Unemployment insurance taxes were reduced by an equal amount.)

An employer and the union (if any) submit a training proposal to the ETP panel, which is comprised of seven representatives of labor and business. The proposal may target the unemployed and/or those current employees who are in danger of losing their jobs. (About 80 percent of ETP funding goes to the second group.) Training may take place on the job or in a classroom. Many programs use community college resources. If the plan is accepted, the state reimburses the employer for the cost of the program. But to ensure that the training leads to a job, the state reimburses only for trainees who remain in their jobs for at least 90 days.

A follow-up study found that those in ETP retraining programs increased their earnings by 27 percent, and by as much as 76 percent for those who were previously unemployed. Over a period of years, unemployment was cut in half for program participants. And the report estimates that their increased earnings and subsequent spending have generated more than a sixfold return to the state.[30]

Individual employers also benefit from California's program. California's Pacific Bell, like the rest of the U.S. telecommunications industry, is introducing new technologies and restructuring work at a rapid pace. With help from ETP and from the Communications Workers of America (CWA), the union that represents the workers, the company is taking steps to retain its work force during this process. The contract between Pacific Bell and CWA guarantees job security and retraining opportunities to current employees. "It is Pacific Bell's policy," states the contract, "to offer to all employees who continue to meet performance standards employment security through re-assignment and re-training even if their present jobs are eliminated."

"We'd come to the conclusion that it would be hard to get employees to work for cost improvements without that [job] security," explains labor relations chief Robert Eastwood.[31]

Since 1986, more than 1,000 employees have been prepared for new jobs. Technicians learn computer maintenance and repair, telephone installers learn how to operate a new digital switching system, and clerical workers learn to be service representatives. Employees earn more money in their new positions, and program costs are paid by the company's $15 million retraining fund and by supplemental funds provided by ETP and administered by CWA.

While state efforts, such as those made in California, go a long way toward easing the job loss and preparing workers for the requirements of new jobs, workplace efforts have also been made. In-house retraining is a cost-effective strategy for an expanding company, but it is not enough in a declining industry. Thus, an agreement between the United Auto Workers union and the three big automakers retrains industrial workers for new jobs, either in the same firm or in different industries.

In 1982, after having suffered the loss of almost 250,000 jobs, the UAW negotiated a groundbreaking agreement with the Chrysler, Ford, and General Motors, in which the employers agreed to contribute to an education and training fund at a rate based on the total number of employee hours per year. The 1987 and 1988 contracts set the rate at between 18 and 19 cents for each hour worked—$1.25 for each hour of overtime above an established level. Under the program, administered jointly by union and management, current or laid-off workers with more than one year's seniority are entitled to tuition assistance, job counseling and placement, and a host of other services.

In addition, each company funds a national center to develop training programs and local services. GM's eight regional Skill Development and Training centers have served tens of thousands of dislocated workers, 80 percent of whom have been placed in new jobs.

A clause in the 1987 and 1988 union contract protects workers from unemployment caused by plant closings, outsourcing, or technological change. (A decline in sales is the only legitimate cause for layoffs.) To compete, the companies will be forced to restructure and automate. Retraining the current work force will thus become more and more critical. In recent years, the training program has been used increasingly to retrain current workers. At Ford, where layoffs have decreased, three-quarters of all participants are now current employees.

Such education and training programs can be carried out by a public employer as well. In New York City, the Board of Education operates a similar training fund available to school maintenance staffs. Based on an 8-cents-per-hour contribution, the Training and Education Fund provides $130,000 a year in scholarships to eligible workers, the members of SEIU Local 74. The program also gives unskilled workers an opportunity to learn new skills and to get a better job.

These efforts are prime examples of successful policies designed and implemented to benefit workers and employers. But much more needs to be done to reach the millions of workers who will be threatened with displacement in the future.

Many displaced workers live in communities with high unemployment. Without time to prepare, most spend long periods out of work. Large numbers of blacks, Hispanics, and older workers simply drop out of the work force in despair (table 6.2).

Table 6.2: Percent of Displaced Workers, by Groups

	Still Looking for Work	Quit Labor Force	Total Unemployed
All displaced workers	17.8	15.3	33.1
Women	16.2	24.1	40.3
Blacks	29.2	13.1	42.3
Hispanics	27.2	16.1	43.3
Older workers (55-64 years)	17.6	35.0	52.6

Note: Data are based on the January 1986 experience of 5.1 million displaced workers with at least three years' job tenure.

Source: BLS, *Displaced Workers, 1981-85*, Bulletin 2289, September 1987.

The mismatch between job seekers and job opportunities has other facets as well. While inner-city unemployment remains high, suburban service jobs go unfilled. Regional disparities are so

pronounced that some observers talk of a "bicoastal economy."
Throughout the 1980s, job growth was concentrated on the East
and West coasts while unemployment was high in the industrial
heartland, the farm belt, and the energy-dependent states. Public
action is needed to help job seekers relocate to areas of job growth
and to stimulate job creation in areas of high unemployment.

Demographers predict slow labor force growth over the next 20
years. Nine out of 10 people who will be working in the year 2000,
they say, are already in the labor force today. In the future,
employers will not be able to rely on new entrants to fill new jobs.
Unless they invest in retraining, they will be forced either to replace
workers with machines or to use only those technologies that match
the limited capabilities of a low-skilled work force. Millions of
American workers will be stuck with second-rate jobs—or no jobs
at all—and the vast potential of information-age technology to
increase productivity and the quality of service will be squandered.

There is a better way.

Solutions

Although change has meant displacement and misery for many
U.S. workers, a renewed commitment to investing in human
resources can help the United States meet the challenges of the
future, regain industrial competitiveness, and promote the well-
being of the new work force. What is needed is a comprehensive
system of lifelong learning—a system based in schools, workplaces, and job training institutions, and funded through a com-
bination of private and public sources.

An ideal system ought to coordinate education, training, employment, and economic development programs. At its foundation
would be economic policies that stimulate job creation and regional
growth. A one-stop nationally coordinated, locally based employment and training agency could be established to coordinate
employment and training needs with economic development
resources and strategies. An industrial extension service, modeled

after the Agriculture Extension Service, could provide technical assistance to small employers in adopting new technologies, training workers, and leveraging public and private resources to promote business development. The U.S. Employment Service (ES), which currently provides job listings for only a small proportion of all job openings (mostly low-skilled ones), could become more aggressive in linking job seekers with employers in an effort to stimulate local economies, as is done in West Germany. A federal employer tax could fund the program. In Delaware, for instance, the Blue Collar Jobs Act is funded through a 0.1 percent tax on employers, and as was previously noted, California's ETP is similarly funded.

Welfare-to-work and dislocated workers programs are components of this larger employment and training system.

The policies of the Swedish National Labor Board provide a model of a comprehensive approach to training and economic development. Since the 1950s, the board has served as an employment service, unemployment insurance program, economic development agency, and training program all wrapped up in one. Local boards, composed of representatives from business, labor, and government, design local job training, placement, relocation, and job creation programs.

By putting economic growth and labor market planning under one roof, the board can take direct steps to avert unemployment by stimulating economic growth and job creation. In a region with high unemployment, for example, it can either offer wage subsidies to attract new industries or pay relocation expenses to help workers move to a different community. The board can create public jobs, promote early retirement programs, or provide investment incentives to businesses. In times of growth, the board can plan for potential labor shortages and initiate worker training programs before problems occur. Three percent of the Swedish labor force is enrolled in retraining programs at any one time.

The national commitment to retraining in Sweden creates a climate in which workers are unlikely to resist technological advances. They can be confident that new technology will lead to new job opportunities, not to unemployment. Moreover, since wage differentials are limited across occupations and industries, Swedish workers in declining manufacturing industries tend to be more willing than U.S. factory workers to retrain for new jobs because they know they will not face large cuts in wages and benefits.

The bottom line is that Sweden maintains a highly productive, high-wage economy with a 1 percent unemployment rate.

A more comprehensive system like the ones described above may not be achievable in our immediate future, but as the United States moves toward it, there are immediate programs we can expand and/or adopt to help train and retrain workers. Creative workplace and public programs that have been pioneered here and abroad point to important new directions in job training and retraining, assistance for displaced workers, career development, and education.

Interim Proposals: Job Training and Retraining

Model state and workplace programs point the way to a public-private partnership that integrates training and retraining with job creation and retention programs.

Establish fully funded federal job training programs. The first step is to reform the current JTPA program to better target the disadvantaged and to provide real training opportunities. Reforms are needed to set performance standards that reward serving the hard-core unemployed and to improve the monitoring of employers who receive federal subsidies to tie placements to long-term, meaningful employment. The new programs should emphasize job retention efforts and make funds available for projects like the one piloted by 9to5 that offer job survival skills training before placement and follow-up support to trainees once they find jobs. Funding levels should be increased for basic and remedial education as well as for high-tech and job-specific training.

Provide comprehensive welfare-to-work programs. As with other programs to help move the low-skilled unemployed into the labor force, the goal should be not just the reduction of the welfare rolls but meaningful job opportunities. Key elements of a welfare employment program include (1) training and education services (including basic education, training for specific jobs, and higher education); (2) job placement assistance; (3) supportive services, including child care, health care, transportation, and other work expenses; (4) voluntary participation, since not all welfare recipients are able to enter the work force; and (5) pay at market rates.

Integrate the employment services program into welfare-to-work reforms. Employment services should be integrated into welfare-to-work programs since these workers know best the local labor markets and are equipped to do job searches and to coordinate education and training activities aimed at providing welfare recipients with real jobs.

Expand state job training programs. Establishment of state-operated job training programs along the lines of the California ETP should be encouraged. Earmarked training taxes collected through the unemployment insurance system are an option, but they should not endanger the financial condition of state unemployment trust funds. Subsidies for retraining workers in-house to meet new jobs should be given priority. Massachusetts' new Health Security Act provides additional funds to retrain workers facing hospital closures for new jobs in expanding health sectors.

Implement workplace job training programs. Much can be done at the workplace even without government support through the establishment of joint labor/management education and training committees. The experiences of Pacific Bell and the UAW cited in this chapter are prime examples.

Worksite training programs can teach occupational skills (medical terminology or computer programming), basic education (literacy or English as a second language), and job search skills (test taking, resume preparation, and career planning). The federal government can encourage such efforts by retaining the tax deductibility of education assistance programs and by providing adequate levels of seed money for joint labor/management programs at individual worksites. In addition, government funding can be used to expand apprenticeship programs that provide essential on-the-job training and prepare workers for future job openings.

Integrate the community college system with business training needs. Today, 66 percent of all community college enrollment is in vocational programs. The community colleges have developed many of these programs in concert with local businesses to train and retrain workers. These partnerships could be expanded with additional state and federal funding. Encouraging the establishment of a coordinated, on-the-job training programs supplemented by formal education acquired through the community college system allows workers to maintain income while enhancing their future job prospects.

Interim Proposals: Assistance to Displaced Workers

Fully funded job programs and retraining subsidies for employers would provide displaced workers with the means to reskill and to enhance their mobility. But as industries and occupations change even more rapidly, these workers need special assistance in preparing for change and minimizing the negative impact of displacement.

Enact state and federal laws requiring employers to notify workers and negotiate over changes in technology and staffing. Advance notification and joint planning help workers and employers prepare for change while taxpayers save money in reduced unemployment benefits, medical assistance, and other public costs.

Implement rapid response teams. Programs such as the Canadian Industrial Adjustment Service minimize the impact of plant closings and major layoffs. The IAS is a popular voluntary federal program in which 95 percent of companies facing layoffs elect to participate. When a company with 50 or more employees must close down or lay off workers, an IAS team moves in quickly to provide training, job search assistance, and other supportive services, and to work with communities on economic development and job creation strategies. The service virtually pays for itself by shortening the duration of unemployment by an average of two weeks.[32]

Expand state employment service (ES) departments. ES offices, part of the unemployment compensation system, are the first point of contact for most dislocated workers, and ES personnel have "hands-on" knowledge of their needs. With increased resources for placement, ES staff could analyze worker needs and provide counseling and referral services. Expanded labor market exchange functions should include research on job trends and better coordination with local businesses and economic development needs.

Provide comprehensive unemployment and training programs. Public programs should provide training, job counseling, skill assessment, and job placement assistance for dislocated workers. Laws that make it difficult for workers to collect unemployment compensation while being retrained should be repealed. (Federal law does permit payment of UI to workers who are enrolled in state-approved training programs, but not all states have such programs.)

Expand short-term compensation programs. Twelve states have experimented with part-time unemployment insurance programs under which firms can reduce their full-time employees to part time and the workers can collect unemployment benefits for the lost hours. During periods of temporary downturns, short-term compensation provides an alternative to layoffs.

Initiate a loan program for displaced workers to assist with retraining, relocation, and business start-up expenses. The student loan program has proven a cost effective way to improve income levels. Other loan programs for dislocated workers could have similar payoffs. Loan repayments could be tied to future earnings levels.

Interim Proposals: Education

Improvements in public education are essential to building the highly skilled work force needed in a changing and competitive world economy. Public policies should achieve the following:

Increase funding for public schools. Adequate funding for a quality educational system, including improved pay and working conditions for teachers and other school employees, should be ensured. In addition, programs to help "at risk" poor children, such as Chapter 1 remedial education assistance, Head Start, and bilingual education, should be funded at levels sufficient to enroll every eligible child.

Maintain and extend funding for low-interest student loan programs. Budget cuts have denied a higher education to many young people in the United States because of lack of funds. A program modeled on the Social Security payroll tax system would allow students to receive government-guaranteed loans that would be repaid through the mandatory withholding of a fixed percentage of income once the borrower got a job. The percentage would depend on the size of the loan, but the withholding would continue throughout most borrowers' working lives, regardless of the amount of the loan or length of employment. Such a program would insulate student loan programs from the annual federal budget battles.

Develop a vocational education system that includes on-the-job apprenticeships. Such programs provide state-of-the-art training and essential work experience, and ease the transition into the labor force for noncollege-bound youth. In West Germany, a three-year apprenticeship program integrates basic education, vocational training, and job experience. Every student in the program attends weekly classes at a vocational school and also works in a company under the tutelage of a master apprentice. State and federal government funding supports the vocational schools; participating companies fund most of the on-the-job training; and apprentices receive a small stipend. In 1986, West German companies invested $13.8 billion in these programs alone—nearly one-third the total training budget for U.S. corporations.[33]

Case Studies

Training Creates Promotion Opportunities for City Employees

For years, city employees in Boston, Mass., complained of being stuck in dead-end jobs. In 1984, SEIU Local 285 determined through a survey that, rather than promoting from within, the city of Boston was recruiting outside applicants to fill many high-paid positions, especially those requiring word processing skills.

With $25,000 a year in career development funds from the city, the 10,000 member union now offers free word processing courses to city workers. Participants receive paid leave for half the time they spend in class, unpaid leave for the other half. The Boston Business School provides the training to classes of 30 students.

More than 400 employees have enrolled, including a larger number of high school dropouts. "The city fills many word processing slots with program applicants," says Nancy Mills, executive director of Local 285, "and the workers feel tremendous pride in their success."

The next step, Mills says, is to give trainees more information about moving up in the city employment system. "There are so many city buildings and so many different jobs," she says, "that many employees don't know where to go for a promotion. We want to work with the city to design a chart that includes all the jobs, the skills they require, and the training needed to move from one position to another."

Welfare Reform in Massachusetts: The Employment and Training Choices Program

Between 1983 and 1988, over 50,000 people got jobs through the Massachusetts Employment and Training Choices Program. The jobs—some full time, some part time—pay an average of $6.50 an hour, or $13,500 a year; 80 percent provide health benefits.

"A commitment to daycare," says Thomas Glynn of the Massachusetts Department of Public Welfare, "is essential to the success of the program." About half the total program budget of $80 million, in fact, goes to child care expenses. Participants receive child care and transportation subsidies while in training and for one year after job placement.

When the program began, federal law did not require welfare recipients with children under age six to participate in a work program. Yet in Massachusetts, 57 percent of all participants are women in this category. They participate because they want to, and because of the child care subsidy, they can afford to do so.

The program allows participants a choice of four programs: career planning, education and training, supported work (the state pays health and other benefits), or immediate job placement. One-third of participants choose to go directly to a job, one-third to skills training, and the rest to either supported work or adult education.

Participants who are working earn twice as much as those who stay on welfare. The main goal of the program "is to help people get out of poverty, not to reduce the welfare caseload," says Glynn. He notes, however, that since the program began, state welfare rolls have declined by 6 percent, the average length of stay on welfare is down 27 percent, and the number of families that remain on welfare more than five years is down 34 percent.

Community Organization and Employer Team Up

Twenty years ago, after a long, hot summer of urban unrest, Bank of America decided to shut down its branch in the Watts section of Los Angeles. But rather than close down the building, a bank employee persuaded managers to turn the facility over to the Los Angeles Urban League for use as a place to teach information processing skills to young people. The need was clear: if unemployment in Watts was high, youth unemployment was even higher. The experiment took off when IBM agreed to provide staff and equipment.

Today, the Los Angeles Urban League program is still operating, and the National Urban League operates similar centers in 35 cities, 29 of them with the assistance of IBM. The League is responsible for recruiting, counseling, and job placement; the company provides equipment and sometimes the training staff. Many of the programs are partially funded by the federal JTPA as well.

The centers graduate about 2,000 students a year, with an 80 percent placement rate. Starting salaries average $12,000 a year. All participants must have a high school degree; most are young black women, many of them mothers.

IBM has invested $11 million in 67 training centers operated in conjunction with community-based organizations. The company estimates that in 1985, participants increased their earnings by $35 million, paid $11 million in taxes, and saved the public $7.4 million in public assistance.

Training Low-Income Women for Clerical Jobs: The Office of the Future Program in New York City

In 1985, a business-labor advisory group took a long, hard look at training programs for clerical workers in New York City and found that the programs fell far short of preparing workers for today's office jobs. Instead of imparting computer literacy that would allow a trainee to use a variety of machines, they taught them only how to operate a single type of word processor. This left the graduates ill-prepared for the fast pace of technological change. Further, many participants couldn't keep up. Lacking basic skills, they needed remedial education before they could go on to learn specific office skills.

Armed with these findings, the Private Industry Council—the business-labor group that manages federal JTPA grants—designed a 26-week training program titled "Office of the Future." The program includes remedial instruction in basic skills: word processing (both generic and specific) and cognitive skills development (in problem solving, independent thinking, organizational behavior, and the like). Graduates are placed in firms that pay a minimum of $18,000 a year, and participating companies make a commitment to send current employees for retraining.

In addition, in 1984, the New York City PIC opened a learning center to provide 120 hours of intensive remedial education in reading and math to trainees who needed it. "Without this training, some of our trainees were getting jobs that they couldn't hold onto," says Vivian Manning Fox, executive director. "They were not able to adapt to the changing office environment." The PIC also runs a keyboard skills training center tailored to the needs of the banking industry.

9to5 Job Retention Project

No one knows the long-term job retention rates of participants in JTPA-funded training programs because follow-up is done only for 90 days. However, anecdotal evidence suggests that many trainees lose jobs for reasons other than lack of work skills. People quitting because they fear being fired; people being fired or walking out because of conflicts with co-workers; people dropping out because of the pressures of juggling work and family—these are all common stories among training agencies.

In fall 1987, 9to5 piloted a Job Retention Project in Milwaukee to provide the missing link between employment and training. The program, which established linkages with seven JTPA-funded clerical training agencies, provides job survival skills to trainees before placement. Participants learn how to manage time and stress, how to ask for help, how to deal with difficult people, and how to identify channels of communication on the job.

9to5's Job Retention Project also follows up on trainees after they find employment to help them identify options when problems arise. In the first year, more than 400 women participated in the project. At least 10 percent stayed on a job they might have left. Some of these were women who received assistance with summer care for school-aged children thanks to the efforts of 9to5.

The project has won strong praise from participants, trainers, employers, and public officials. In a letter of appreciation, Milwaukee County Executive Dave Schulz wrote, "The obstacles many new entrants face in adapting to the realities of the workplace can be frustrating, but your program goes a long way in showing that they are not insurmountable."

Employers have introduced a range of techniques, including drug testing, polygraphs, and electronic surveillance, which increase management control and reduce employees' privacy and autonomy. Under these conditions, the fuel that drives employee performance is not commitment to do good work—it's stress.

—Harley Shaiken, University of California, San Diego

You don't have to think that much because the computer is doing that for you. People here have begun to feel like monkeys.

—Benefits analyst in a large insurance company, quoted in Shoshana Zuboff, *In the Age of the Smart Machine: The Future of Work and Power.*

Immediately after we moved into the new building, people began to experience nausea, skin irritation, burning eyes. I went home practically every night with a headache, completely exhausted. Eventually, researchers discovered that the building had been built on a site that was polluted with chemicals. Whenever it rained, the chemicals seeped into the basement. The ventilation system was so bad that pollutants were trapped inside the building. But it was too late for me. My right lung was already seriously infected with a rare fungus that lived in the ventilation system. Most of my lung had to be removed.

—Phil Thornton, Department of Human Services, Caribou, Maine.

Chapter 7:
Working Conditions: Health and Safety, Dignity and Autonomy on the Job

The emerging service economy holds out the promise of clean, safe workplaces, free of the hazards of mine and factory. And computer technology opens up the possibility that machines will take over mundane tasks and free workers for more creative and productive work. But reality falls far short of this promise.

"Twentieth century technology is being used to recreate the nineteenth-century sweatshop," says Harley Shaiken, author of *Work Transformed: Automation and Labor in the Computer Age.* "Computers are being used for monitoring and control rather than expanding employees' autonomy and satisfaction." When employers use computers to break down complex tasks into routine, repetitive operations, problems emerge. The electronic sweatshop is rife with boredom, fatigue, health problems, stress, and low morale and motivation.

Computer technology has spread well beyond the office setting into hundreds of occupations. Truck drivers, lab technicians, and nurses, as well as secretaries and telephone operators, all work with computers. Gas meter readers log on to a computer in their truck at the beginning of their route. The computer then tracks every second of their day, from how long it takes to read a meter to the time between calls and the time spent in the truck billing each customer. "We used to exercise independent judgment and considerable freedom on our route," says an employee of East Ohio Gas Company in Cleveland. "Now the computer monitors every minute of our day."

New technology could be used to reorganize work so as to allow workers to exercise more judgment and to make jobs more stimulating and more rewarding. Instead, most employers use computers to increase their control not just over what their employees do, but also over exactly how they do it. In place of good management, they use electronic monitoring to recreate the assembly line in service jobs. In addition, they use drug tests and polygraphs to control rather than to supervise workers. In sum, new technology allows them to watch over their workers' every move.

"These techniques may lead to a short-term increase in productivity," Shaiken acknowledges. "But in the long run, there is a hidden cost in the quality of service, morale, and often the health of the work force."

Indeed, the hazards of service jobs now rank alongside those of industrial work as a major threat to worker health and safety. But the new dangers do not receive the recognition they deserve. Unlike industrial accidents, the hazards faced by secretaries, health care workers, janitors, social workers, and policemen are often difficult to detect and may take years to surface. While federal and state laws now regulate health and safety for industrial workers and miners, few regulations protect service workers from indoor air pollution, exposure to asbestos, infectious diseases, video display terminal syndrome, and stress. And federal occupational health and safety laws do not protect state and municipal workers. In the 26 states that lack occupational safety and health laws, public employees have no legal guarantee of a safe workplace.

If we can learn one lesson from our industrial past, it should be this: all society suffers when workers are forced to sacrifice their right to dignity, privacy, and a safe and healthy workplace.

Government action was required to establish standards in industrial workplaces. Today, new standards are required to protect employees' rights to privacy, dignity, and safety in the service economy.

Surveillance on the Job

Computer Monitoring

Four to six million employees—truck drivers, lab technicians, word processors, data entry clerks, customer service representatives, telephone operators—have their performance at work evaluated by data provided by computer monitoring.[1] Managers claim that monitoring sets objective standards, raises productivity, and improves performance. In fact, monitoring undermines workers' ability to work productively while harming their health and morale.

To being with, monitoring undermines the quality of service. Managers claim that it allows them to ensure accuracy and good customer service—"to ensure," in the words of an airline industry spokesperson, "that customers are being treated in a polite way and are being given accurate information."[2]

But the pressure to meet production quotas often requires workers to provide inferior service. In one large insurance company, for example, nonmonitored employees told researchers that their priority was accuracy in processing, but monitored employees said their priority was the volume of claims processed.[3] At Pacific Southwest Airlines, airline reservation agents complain that they "don't have time to wait on our customers." They are allowed 120 seconds per phone call, 11 seconds between calls. The computer keeps track of who is falling behind. Those who can't keep up are fired.[4] And telephone operators at Southwestern Bell in Independence, Mo., are permitted 20 seconds per phone call. "If an operator spends too much time with a customer, she is in trouble," says one employee. "Because so little time is allowed to assist customers, operators occasionally may provide the customer with the wrong phone number."[5]

The speed-up that often accompanies monitoring may lead to short-term productivity gains, but for many employers, the long-term decline in morale is costly. The machines that replace personal interactions between managers and workers can't motivate workers, understand employee problems, or foster loyalty.

Second, monitoring is a major factor contributing to stress on the job. A 1980 study by the National Institute of Occupational Safety and Health (NIOSH) found a greater degree of depression, anxiety, instability, fatigue, and anger among heavily monitored employees than among those who weren't monitored.[6] Similarly, a 1984 national survey on women and stress found that high stress levels were more common among electronically monitored workers than among nonmonitored ones.[7] "We were told last week that we failed to meet management productivity goals," a data entry clerk wrote. "I feel so depressed, my stomach is in knots, I take tons of aspirin, my jaws are sore from clenching my teeth, I'm so tired I can't get up in the morning, and my arm hurts from entering, entering, entering."

Speed-up often results from computer monitoring, and that also heightens worker stress. At Digital Equipment Corporation in Atlanta, Ga., quotas for customer service representatives went up from 14 calls per day to 30 calls after monitoring began.[8]

Third, monitoring invades workers' and customers' privacy. Computers can be programmed to collect information about workers that is unrelated to productivity. Supervisors can push a button in another room and overhear phone calls and private conversations without notifying the worker or customer. A reservation agent with Pacific Southwest Airlines testified at a California state hearing that she was disciplined for a comment she made to a co-worker between telephone calls. Her employer, she said, was eavesdropping by computer.

In the future, employers may be able to use new technologies developed for use by defense intelligence agencies that pick up key phrases from telephone conversations. If such technologies were to enter the workplace, an employer could detect a worker's religious or political involvement, union activity, or personal problems.

Fourth, performance evaluation based on computer monitoring is unfair. Managers say computer monitoring provides an objective means of evaluating performance. "It's a way to establish what a fair day's work should be," says one management consultant. And initially, some workers welcome monitoring for this reason. But they change their minds as they rarely have an opportunity to challenge computer inaccuracies or explain special circumstances, and as they discover that the data is used as much to stimulate competition and speed-up as to help them do their jobs better.

In most telephone companies, for example, individual performances rates are posted for all employees to see. Such a practice hurts employee morale, causes stress, and may actually do little to improve the quality or quantity of work. A group of 100 telephone operators in Tempe, Ariz., posted group averages instead of individual rates. Productivity and quality went up.[9]

Drug Testing

Since 1982, employers have dramatically increased the practice of random drug testing. In Fortune 500 firms, drug testing increased tenfold (from 3 to 30 percent) between 1982 and 1985.[10] Federal agencies have been ordered to establish random testing programs; up to 1.1 million workers will be affected. State and local governments have also stepped up testing, particularly of law enforcement officials, security guards, and transportation workers. All too often these testing programs trample workers' rights and focus on punishment rather than on treatment of substance abusers.

Why the drug testing frenzy? Employers argue that drug tests control drug abuse on the job, protect public safety, reduce absenteeism, and lower health care costs. Many elected officials support drug testing to bolster an "antidrug" public image. But the facts show that random testing is not an effective solution to drug use in the workplace.

For one thing, drug tests can be highly inaccurate. Accuracy depends on the type of test used, the quality of laboratory use, and the skill of the person performing the test. Many drug tests, especially those used in initial screening, have a very high error rate. Unlike tests for alcohol in the bloodstream, they measure not the active ingredient but inactive by-products. Traces of herbal teas, poppy seeds, and over-the- counter drugs found in the urine can yield false positive results.

In addition, many legal experts insist that employers do not have the legal right to extract bodily substances, such as blood or urine, from an employee's body—that such tests are the ultimate invasion of privacy. Urine samples taken for drug testing have been illegally examined for other purposes as well. In Washington, D.C., for example, urine samples from female police applicants were used without permission to test not just for drug use but also for pregnancy.[11]

Certainly, employers have a legitimate interest in judging an employee's ability to work productively and safely. But while drug tests can indicate impairment on the job, more often they reveal the long-past use of drugs *off* the job. As a result, the employer is attempting to control workers actions beyond the time that the employee is at work.

Another objection is that drug tests are too often punitive, not treatment oriented. "We have district commanders who will require an officer to take a drug screen simply because they don't like him," reports a member of the Chicago Fraternal Order of Police.[12] Punitive drug testing programs make workers shy away from employee assistance programs designed to help them with alcohol or drug abuse problems.

Finally, such tests do not tell anything about employee performance. Thus, they are no substitute for good management and supervision. An employer shouldn't need to perform drug tests to establish which employees perform poorly or take too much time off.

The battle over drug testing will be fought in the courts. Several circuit court cases have ruled that public employees are protected against random drug testing under the Fourth Amendment, which guarantees protection against "unreasonable search and seizure" by the federal government, and under the Fourteenth Amendment, which extends this protection to state and local employees. Other courts have issued contrary rulings. The Supreme Court is expected to rule in 1988 on drug testing cases involving customs officials and railroad employees. Meanwhile, the National Labor Relations Board has issued guidelines advising employers that, in any case, they may not impose drug testing without consulting the union.

Polygraphs

Federal law now limits the use of lie detectors by most private employers. But the law exempts public employers, drug companies, private security firms and other consultants to security agencies, and any other employers who are investigating theft.

For example, polygraphs are widely used in the jewelry industry to guard against theft. "Fear of theft is a legitimate concern," says Joe Tarantola, president of SEIU Local 1-J. "But proper supervision and inspection are more effective than invading workers' privacy." Thus, when two jewelry workers were fired for refusing to take a lie detector test in 1976, the union filed a grievance. Arbitrator Jay Kramer ruled in favor of the union, asserting that not only are polygraphs highly inaccurate, but they also violate constitutional provisions against self-incrimination and unreasonable search and seizure, and for the right to confront and cross-examine one's accusers.

"Employers continued to request that workers submit to the tests," says Tarantola. "But many of our members refused." Before the federal ban on polygraphs took effect in 1988, about 2 million workers and job applicants were required to take lie detector tests each year. And because the ban exempts employers who are investigating theft, some employers may continue to try to force jewelry workers to take the tests. But according to a 1983 study by the congressional Office of Technology Assessment, polygraphs can be wrong more than half the time.[13]

Nor are they a reliable tool for screening job applicants. "Exceptionally honest and intelligent individuals may be highly reactive to questions about truthfulness," explains Dr. Leonard Saxe, author of the OTA study. "Such desirable employees will be misidentified at higher rates than other less desirable employees."[14]

Finally, polygraphs may also reveal highly personal information about family problems, sexual preference, personal habits, and political beliefs. Workers need to be protected against such broad assaults on their right to privacy.

AIDS

AIDS or HIV testing is the next frontier for employers. AIDS testing may be used as a precondition to obtain employment or health insurance or as an excuse to discriminate against groups on the basis of lifestyles. But to use it in such a way violates civil liberties and does not promote the health concern of the public. Testing for AIDS should be offered to those who want it but only on a voluntary basis.

The AIDS testing frenzy often singles out teachers, health care workers, and patients as candidates for testing. But health care workers are themselves at risk of contracting AIDS from exposure to contaminated needles, blood, and other bodily fluids in the course of caring for patients. Health care workers need universal precautions to protect them from such exposures, not AIDS testing.

Health and Safety

Three out of four U.S. workers are employed in service sector workplaces such as offices, schools, and retail stores. These job sites are home to a host of physical and psychological hazards—namely, video display terminals, indoor air pollution, asbestos, infectious disease, and stress.

Video Display Terminal (VDT) Syndrome

More than 28 million Americans use VDTs on the job, and the number could rise to 40 million in just a few years, according to the National Academy of Sciences.[15] And a growing body of evidence shows that all these people are at risk. Recent studies document a direct correlation between VDT use and vision problems, muscle strain, fatigue, chronic headaches, and other stress-related conditions. A 1986 survey by the Data Entry Management Association found that 66 percent of data-entry operators suffered neck and shoulder pain, 47 percent had burning eyes, and 44 percent experienced blurred vision.[16] The more time spent at the terminal, the higher the rate of health problems.[17]

VDT workers can also develop carpal-tunnel syndrome, a disabling nerve condition caused by the strain of constantly repeating hand or wrist motions. Meatcutters, postal workers, and seamstresses are also vulnerable to this disorder.

Some evidence suggests that VDT use during pregnancy may harm fetal development. A 1988 study of nearly 1,600 pregnant women who worked more than 20 hours per week on a VDT found they had twice the miscarriage rate of other women office workers.[18] The cause of the problem—radiation from the terminal, stress, or something entirely different—is unknown. However, two animal studies found higher rates of birth defects in pregnant animals exposed to VDT-type radiation,[19] and anecdotal evidence of birth defects among the children of VDT users is additional cause for caution and further research.

Another survey of hundreds of VDT operators by 9to5, National Association of Working Women, finds reproductive problems to be high among VDT operators. Of those who had become pregnant since working on a VDT, 31.6 percent reported normal births and 30.6 percent suffered miscarriages. Normally, between 10 percent and 20 percent of all pregnancies end in miscarriage.[20]

During the past several years, at least 25 states and many other jurisdictions have considered legislation to guarantee safe working conditions for VDT operators. Below are two examples of successful initiatives in this regard.

—Suffolk County, N.Y., is the first jurisdiction to require comprehensive health and safety protections for VDT operators in both the public and the private sector. The 1988 law which is being currently contested in the courts requires employees who work at least 26 hours per week on VDTs to be provided with detachable keyboards, adjustable furniture, and proper lighting in all workplaces with 20 or more VDTs. A 15-minute rest break is required for every 3 hours of VDT work, and employers must provide yearly eye examinations for VDT operators when needed. The law also establishes a commission to review the law every two years and propose revisions based on new research and technology.

—In 1987, the governor of New York State promulgated a policy for 10,000 state VDT workers requiring flexible workstations, proper lighting, glare control, noise control, machine maintenance, and work breaks. In addition, supervisors of VDT operators are directed to improve "job design" by providing greater variety, flexibility, and worker input into planning and decision making.

Indoor Air Pollution

As many as 20 percent of all buildings exhibit "sick building syndrome." Many of the office buildings built after the energy crisis of the 1970s are hermetically sealed to admit little fresh air. As a result, inside air becomes polluted with toxic fumes: carbon monoxide exhaust from indoor parking garages or loading docks, ozone from photocopying machines, formaldehyde and solvents in furniture and carpets, cigarette smoke, and micro-organisms in poorly maintained ventilation systems.

—Soldiers living in modern barracks where the windows do not open have twice as many respiratory problems as soldiers in old barracks.[21]

—A survey involving 3,400 state employees and hundreds of work sites in New Hampshire and Maine found complaints of nausea, headaches, eye irritation, and skin rashes concentrated at certain sites. Clearly, specific buildings—not just individual workers—are the source of the problem.[22]

"The estimated probability of suffering a fatal disease is substantially higher for exposure to indoor air pollutants than for exposure to the pollutants in outdoor air, drinking water and food," according to a recent report in *Scientific American*.[23] Correcting the problem is sometimes as simple and inexpensive as increasing fresh air intake or cleaning dirty ventilation ducts. Yet employers are slow to respond to employee complaints, and in the absence of government regulation, employees continue to toil in unhealthy buildings.

Asbestos

Of all the hazardous material used in building construction, none is more notorious than asbestos. Tiny filaments, unknowingly inhaled, do not naturally decompose. Even small doses can cause fatal lung cancer and mesothelioma, a form of cancer unique to asbestos victims; larger doses can cause asbestosis, a scarring of the lungs. Since the asbestos problem first came to light in the late 1970s, there has been a rash of clumsy and dangerous abatement efforts. An unpublished Environmental Protection Agency (EPA) report noted that faulty abatement in the schools could cost the lives of 1,100 workers.[24]

Aside from an underfunded federal plan aimed at removing asbestos from public schools, no federal standards or programs cover the more than 730,000 public and commercial buildings that contain hazardous asbestos material.[25]

Infectious Diseases

Every year, millions of workers in the fields of health care, public safety, and human services are in direct contact with people suffering from infectious diseases. The federal Centers for Disease

Control have established recommendations designed to provide proper protection and training so that nurses, doctors, social workers, and police officers can continue to provide compassionate care without fear of contracting serious illnesses. But the federal government has failed to make these recommendations legally binding.

Voluntary standards are not enough. Every year, more than 15,000 health care workers contract hepatitis B on the job, and 200 to 300 die from the infection. An SEIU survey in 1988 found that only one-quarter of all health care facilities have procedures to determine which workers are at risk of contracting AIDS or hepatitis B. Fewer than half of the facilities provide training and protective equipment to nurses' aides, housekeeping personnel, and other nonmedical staff. And while a quarter of the facilities fail to vaccinate employees to protect against hepatitis B, of the three-quarters that do, one-third make employees pay to be vaccinated.[26]

To date, only a handful of workers are reported to have contracted the AIDS virus; however, proper training and protective measures are necessary to safeguard all those who work with AIDS patients.

Stress

Stress accounts for 14 percent of all workers' compensation claims. "When the work is more mental than manual,. . .workplace injuries will be, too," reports the *Wall Street Journal*. "Add in computers, which often make tasks repetitive and workloads heavier, and stress experts say more employees will suffer 'technostress'."[27]

Job-related stress is not a figment of workers' imagination. It can result in everyday symptoms—headaches, stomach aches, insomnia, diarrhea—as well as in serious illnesses—asthma, ulcers, colitis, and hypertension. It is caused by concrete conditions at the workplace.

NIOSH lists the following as major causes of stress at work: work overload, lack of control over one's work, nonsupportive supervisors of co-workers, limited job opportunities, role ambiguity or conflict, rotating shift work, and machine-paced work. Jobs in health care, service occupations, and blue-collar factory work are rated the most stressful.[28] "High demands, low control and a low level of physical exertion are the three major job factors leading to stress-related disease," says Dr. Robert Karasek of the University of Southern California.[29] And in a 1984 survey on women and stress, 9to5 found that the most stress-related medical problems are caused by always being subjected to excessive supervision or monitoring of work and that nonmanagement women, while less likely to describe their work as "very stressful," were more likely to experience the health effects of stress.

A NIOSH study found that health care workers fill 7 of the 27 most stressful occupations.[30] The Framingham Heart Study showed that women clerical workers have twice the rate of coronary heart disease as experienced by other women.[31]

Workplace stress may cost society as much as $150 billion each year, according to a report by the Bureau of National Affairs.[32] And employers who are slow to respond to stress complaints pay a price. When employees have no choice but to work under difficult conditions or quit, productivity declines. Stress accounts for 40 percent of job turnover. And workers' compensation awards for stress-related disease are on the rise, averaging $15,000 a claim.[33]

Solutions

The abusive use of new technology and the rise of hazards in service jobs require new policies to protect workers. A variety of legislation points the way to new national standards.

Autonomy and Job Control: Legislative Actions

Curb electronic surveillance. In many European countries there is *no individual* monitoring. According to the OTA, legislation restricting electronic surveillance is part of broader guidelines "on the rights to health, safety, privacy, constitutional protections, or information that employees can expect to enjoy in the workplace."[34] In Sweden, Norway, Germany, and Holland, employers are required by law to involve workers and their unions in decisions about job design, the introduction of new technology, and other factors affecting the quality of work life. Norwegian law outlaws monotonous work.

In the absence of such comprehensive legislation, both Congress and state governments should take immediate action to outlaw electronic monitoring. Short of that, they should work to eliminate its worst abuses. Steps in this regard should be undertaken based on the following considerations:

—*Right to know.* Require that workers be notified when surveillance occurs; pass a "beep" bill, which requires an audible tone when an employer listens in on a conversation; and provide individuals with access to their personnel files and with full information on how data are collected and used.

—*Right to due process.* Establish procedures to allow employees to appeal data collected by computer.

—*Meaningful standards.* Require measurements to be meaningful and relevant to the work performed.

Oppose random and universal drug testing programs. The focus of any workplace substance abuse program should be treatment, not punishment. The centerpiece of any program should be an employee assistance program designed to promote treatment and rehabilitation. Rhode Island, for example, requires employers with drug testing programs to establish employee assistance programs as well.

Employers who conduct drug tests should see them only as part of a well-integrated plan to combat substance abuse and should thereby provide adequate worker protections. At a minimum, these protections should include (1) treatment referral as the result of initial positive test; (2) guaranteed job return after successful completion of treatment; (3) notification to employees about the tests and the laboratories involved; (4) establishment of an appeals process; (5) guaranteed confidentiality; and (6) accurate testing procedures performed by well-trained professionals.

Ban the use of polygraphs in all workplaces. Recognizing the inaccuracy and questionable constitutionality of lie detector tests, Congress joined 21 states and the District of Columbia in restricting the use of polygraphs by most private employers in 1988. This legislation should be extended to cover public sector workers and employees in private sector occupations that are currently exempt.

Oppose mandatory AIDS testing at the workplace. Testing for HIV should be offered to those who want it but only on a voluntary basis. Testing should be conducted in a setting which guarantees confidentiality, and anonymity if requested. Counseling both before and after testing must also be included as part of any voluntary testing program. Persons with AIDS should be allowed to work as long as they are able do so. Legislation should be passed to extend antidiscrimination protections to those carrying the AIDS virus.

Health and Safety: Legislative Actions

When the Occupational Safety and Health Administration was established in 1970, its focus was the industrial sector; little attention was paid to service sector hazards. However, standards are urgently needed in areas that affect the well-being of millions of service workers.

Establish standards for safe use of video display terminals. New OSHA standards should regulate the use of VDTs in the workplace, requiring regular eye exams; rest breaks; proper lighting; the use of ergonomically designed equipment; and the right of pregnant workers to refuse VDT work. Although a few states and localities have passed such legislation, a federal standard is urgently needed.

Establish indoor air quality standards. Federal and state indoor clean-air regulations should be enacted. As a first step, should establish an Office of Indoor Air Quality within EPA whose mandate is to develop a plan to reduce indoor air pollution and to investigate worker complaints.

Require safe clean-up of asbestos in schools and other buildings.

—Congress should enforce the 1986 Asbestos Hazard Emergency Response Act (AHERA), which sets timetables for asbestos inspection and abatement in all school buildings. Under that law, building service workers and contractors who conduct the clean-up must receive proper training and follow EPA guidelines.

—Congress should provide sufficient funding for the Asbestos School Hazard Abatement Act (ASHAA) to provide schools with the funds and technical assistance needed to detect hazardous asbestos and clean it up.

—Congress should enact legislation requiring EPA to develop regulations for safe and effective abatement of asbestos in other public and commercial buildings. The legislation concerning asbestos in the schools provides a cost-effective, graduated approach that is applicable to the nation's public and commercial buildings, as well. A step-by-step plan might require cleanup of public buildings first, followed by commercial buildings.

Protection from infectious diseases. The Centers for Disease Control recommends the following guidelines to protect workers from exposure to the AIDS virus, hepatitis B, and other bloodborne diseases:

—employees should wear protective clothing—including gowns, gloves, and masks—to guard against exposure;

—needles and other contaminated equipment must be disposed of properly;

—health care facilities must be actively involved in training and monitoring for compliance; and

—exposed workers should receive the hepatitis B vaccine.

OSHA should move quickly to establish permanent standards. All workers who come in contact with blood or other bodily fluids should receive vaccines, training, and protective equipment free of charge.

Expand OSHA to include public employees and increase OSHA funding to enable vigorous enforcement of existing standards.

Expansion of OSHA to include public employees would finally guarantee a safe work environment to those local and state workers in the 26 states without occupational safety and health laws.

Even when protective regulations do exist, it is hard for workers to benefit from them. OSHA enforcement declined dramatically during the Reagan years; the number of inspectors dropped by 20 percent and workplace injuries went up. Many employers seemed to find it more cost-effective to take the small risk of being fined than to eliminate hazards from the workplace. (OSHA fines are only $1,000 for a serious violation and $10,000 for a willful act.)[35]

Stress. All states should include stress as a condition covered by workers' compensation. In addition, policymakers should support initiatives to alleviate stress on the job, such as measures to raise pay and benefits; to provide workers with advance notice of technological change, plant closings, and massive layoffs; to improve career opportunities; and to ban electronic monitoring and other forms of employee surveillance.

Autonomy and Job Control, Health and Safety: Workplace Actions

Many employers who have redesigned work to provide autonomy and safe working conditions have reaped rewards in higher morale and increased productivity. Various programs can provide alternatives to surveillance and can protect workers' rights to a safe and healthy work environment.

Labor-management quality of work life committees. Labor-management committees can give workers a voice in the design, structure, and pace of work. When these committees have real authority to transform worker concerns into positive solutions, quality and productivity improve without the need for punitive policies or tight control.

Substitute good supervision for surveillance. Many employers avoid computer monitoring, finding that the costs in stress and low morale outweigh any short-term gains in improved performance. Good supervisors and good work design are by far more effective in boosting productivity and quality service. Where monitoring is used, meaningful standards and appeals procedures should be established.

Monitoring results should not be used to discipline workers.

Establish employee assistance programs to control substance abuse. Helping loyal employees who suffer from substance abuse is a complex but cost-effective process. Many companies, often in conjunction with unions, have employee assistance programs designed to help workers with drug or alcohol abuse problems. These programs focus on treatment rather than on punishment.

Protect workers' right to know and right to act to ensure healthy and safe working conditions. Health and safety regulations are not enough to protect worker safety. Employers must also provide workers with information about the potential hazards, the right to inspect facilities, the right to refuse to work under unsafe or unhealthy conditions, and job protections for whistleblowers who reveal unsafe working conditions to co-workers or the public. Workplace health and safety committees are critical for enforcing laws, discovering new hazards, and providing proper training.

Alleviate the conditions that cause stress. Research shows that employees with a reasonable work load, good supervision, control over the pace and design of work, advancement opportunities, good pay and benefits, clarity of roles and demands, a safe work environment, and avenues to solve problems experience greater job satisfaction and fewer symptoms of stress. Working conditions that provide dignity and autonomy lead to superior job performance as well.

Wellness programs should look at ways to eliminate stress brought on by job design as well as ways to cope.

Case Studies

West Virginia Beeper Bill Curtails Monitoring

West Virginia was the only state in the nation to require employers who listen in on telephone conversations at the workplace to notify both workers and customers when such monitoring is taking place. The West Virginia "beeper" bill, passed in 1981, required employers to (1) sound an audible tone during monitoring; (2) declare in the telephone directory that telephone calls may be monitored; and (3) put stickers on monitored workers' telephones informing them of the practice.

After the law was passed, C&P Telephone, then the AT&T operating company in the state, stopped listening in on telephone operators' conversations with customers. Although many employers claim such eavesdropping is essential to maintain high-quality performance, productivity and service remained excellent without it. In fact, a 1982 AT&T survey of regional telephone companies ranked C&P "outstanding" in customer service and number one in the Bell system in 6 out of 12 categories. During the same period, C&P Telephone transferred a large part of its Washington, D.C., directory assistance operation to West Virginia—another sign that the absence of monitoring was not hurting quality of service.

Despite these positive reports, AT&T announced that it would not build a major new facility in the state while the "beeper" bill was on the books. The legislature repealed the bill in 1986.

Coalition Wins Indoor Air Quality Laws in Northern New England

The sick building in Caribou, Maine, where Phil Thornton lost his lung had its counterparts in other parts of the state. "We were constantly trying to get state inspectors in to look at these buildings," reports Phil Merrill, executive director of the Maine State Employees Association. "But they didn't know what to look for. Or they'd tell the building owners when they were coming, and on inspection day, all of a sudden a flood of fresh air would come pouring into the ventilation system."

Further, the state was without leverage to force employers to clean up their buildings. Indoor air standards existed at neither the state nor the federal level. Therefore, MSEA joined with the State Employees Association of New Hampshire/

SEIU Local 1984 and SEIU in a three-pronged strategy to address the problem.

"First, we had to convince people that the problem was real," says Merrill. "We surveyed workers in every state building in New Hampshire and Maine and found that there was a pattern to workers' complaints about headaches and dizziness. In buildings with air-tight windows, employees were twice as likely to get sick and to complain of headaches." The coalition publicized results to the media, policymakers, and public employees.

Next, the coalition pressed the state administration to train maintenance workers in proper ventilation. Finally, the coalition launched its most ambitious effort: passage of state standards on indoor air pollution. This effort succeeded, and in spring 1988, Maine and New Hampshire became the first states to pass indoor air quality legislation.

—The Maine law requires that all newly constructed or newly leased state buildings meet minimum air quality standards and that the state develop a plan to clean up other state buildings. The state will aim for 20 cubic feet per minute per person of fresh air— the minimum recommended by the American Society of Heating, Refrigeration and Air Conditioning Engineers.

—The New Hampshire law requires that a state building must "meet clean air standards before it may be used for any state purposes, other than storage," and mandates the director of public health services to establish indoor air quality standards.

Labor/Community Coalition Wins
School Asbestos Abatement

For years, janitors complained that they were being asked to clean up asbestos without proper training or equipment—even to pull asbestos off pipes with their bare hands. SEIU also received reports of elevated levels of lung cancer, asbestosis, and deaths from mesothelioma among school cleaners. Workers' compensation claims were slow in coming—sometimes coming too late. A school janitor in Newton, Mass., won his workers' claim only after he died of mesothelioma.

But even after the dangers of asbestos exposure were widely recognized, the federal government failed to require asbestos inspection and safe clean-up. So SEIU developed a two-pronged strategy to force the government to act. First, the union petitioned EPA to establish rules for safe asbestos abatement. Second, it initiated a coalition effort to pressure Congress to require and fund clean and safe abatement in the schools. The National Education Association, the National PTA, and the National School Boards Association joined in.

In August 1984, Congress passed the Asbestos School Hazard Abatement Act (ASHAA), which would release $600 million to assist schools with abatement as soon as EPA ruled that an abatement was required. But the EPA continued to drag its feet.

Meanwhile, haphazard abatement in the schools was endangering more lives. In January 1985, SEIU took the agency to court to force action.

In October 1986, Congress voted unanimous approval for the (School) Asbestos Hazard Emergency Response Act (AHERA), which requires schools to identify and carry out abatement plan. The law also authorizes a federal study of the problem in public and commercial buildings. A week later, SEIU won the lawsuit against EPA, requiring EPA to establish asbestos hazard and abatement standards in schools.

AHERA established guidelines for asbestos cleanup in every U.S. elementary and secondary school, including the following requirements: (1) inspection by an accredited inspector; (2) development of a written management plan; (3) training for school building service workers in asbestos safety; (4) asbestos abatement by certified contractor or supervisor; and (5) air sampling after abatement. A strict timetable for each stage was established, and implementation of the management plan must begin by 12 July 1989.

With the victory in the schools, the next priority is public and commercial buildings.

Chapter 8:
Putting People First: Investment and National Tax and Spending Priorities

The worldwide dominance of mass manufacturing and the economic strength the United States enjoyed following World War II gave us a strategic edge in the world economy. These advantages enabled us to develop a unique social contract in which American business, through negotiations with unions or individual workers, set national policies for wages, hours, health and pension, leave, training, investment, and industrial research and development, with the well-being of the work force promoted as a central corporate goal. Local communities, states and the federal government imposed few constraints and rarely questioned business priorities.

Today, however, the competitive edge we inherited 40 years ago has largely vanished. Europe and Japan have developed and applied advanced technology to a wide variety of industries and are now the home of international corporations capable of squeezing out American industries in worldwide competition. In one industry after another, other advanced industrialized nations are building on new technologies that allow their people to move beyond the sweat labor of mass manufacturing assembly lines toward jobs that require an educated, motivated labor force capable of applying advanced technologies for productivity and quality improvements.

And competition will accelerate in the years ahead. Countries in Europe and Southeast Asia will remain major competitors. Further advances in less developed countries around the world, and the potential entry of the Soviet Union and China into the global marketplace, will intensify the battle for markets and resources into the 1990s.

Virtually all technology and management experts agree that an industrialized nation's labor force—its people—will be a key resource in maintaining global competitiveness in the decades to come. The electronic age gives a strong economic advantage to the nation best able to redesign work and social policies so as to motivate, engage, and stimulate its workers' creative energies.

Throughout this book we have shown how the United States must change direction if it is to keep pace with world leaders and maintain and improve the future for our children. To that effect, we have presented initial public and workplace policy steps toward the writing of a new, stronger social contract between the corporate custodians of our economic resources and the labor force.

But the broad agenda for our nation must also include policies that encourage long-term investment in economic growth, and this means investment in people. We now turn briefly to the broader issues of changing corporate strategies and national tax and spending policies.

Living on Borrowed Time and Money

As we have already discussed, the illusion of economic growth over the last decade has relied largely on families' willingness to work harder for less pay and less health, retirement, or job security. Working people have had fewer children or have even postponed starting a family so as to grapple with the delicate balancing required for work and family concerns.

This illusion has also relied on the nation's ability to go into debt to maintain spending levels. In fact, the United States has swung from being the world's large lender to being the largest debtor nation. The federal budget and national trade deficits have paid for continued national expansion despite stagnant or declining American family incomes. Although these huge deficits have been maintained for years without major visible costs, jointly they threaten our future economic viability.

Time is also running out for American corporations. Labor shortages and the morale and productivity costs that flow from efforts to create a more disposable work force ultimately limit the profits available from wealth redistribution. Similarly, the 1980s' race to profit from the tax breaks flowing from mergers, acquisitions, and leveraged buyouts is yet another short-term redistribution strategy—a shift from the public purse into the pockets of corporate owners.[1] Far from being a blueprint for investment in economic growth, quality, or innovative products or services, these short-term tactics will cause us all to lose out if, as a result of failure to invest, the United States' share of world and domestic markets continues to decline.

As borrowed time and money reach their limits, the United States faces a choice. It can continue on the current path of stagnant income and inequality and be content to sink to a second tier in the world economic hierarchy. Or it can put in place new national spending, tax, and legislative controls that will channel U.S. corporate energy away from wealth redistribution and toward activities that produce growth and a shared wealth for the nation.

In the past, bad management of a company meant losing out in domestic markets to other, better-managed U.S. companies. Today, bad management and short-sighted work policies mean losing out to competitors from abroad, which in turn threatens the nation's standard of living. And at the root of these problems are corporate leaders who are wasting our national resources.

To safeguard their collective future, other countries have taken the lead in developing social policies that view corporate leaders as the custodians rather than the owners of national resources. Europe and Japan, as well as socialist countries, have placed limits on corporate freedom to buy or sell national resources, to move from place to place at will, or to be the sole determinants of social wages through private job policies. If our national goal is a rising standard of living and an improved quality of life, we can no longer afford to leave private business free to set national policies with regard to wages, hours, and working conditions—current policies that only serve to cheapen our work force.

Investing in People: Designing Jobs That Maximize Our Key National Resource

Investment and innovation have always been critical to productivity, quality, and economic growth. In the electronic age, work designs that place a high value on people have emerged as one of the critical investment choices.

Yet the predominant mentality embodied in American business investment strategies is to use technology to displace people and reduce the skill levels of those remaining at work. This bias derives from the success of 1930s-style assembly lines used in mass production of highly standardized products. American business has tried to extend this emphasis on fragmented, specialized, and narrow-skill jobs to an age of "smart" machines. The trend is to "dumb-down" jobs by trying to make work so simple that the people who do it don't have to be able to read, write, add, or even think. In stores, machines do the counting, the adding, the inventory. Pictures on keyboards replace numbers. In offices, managers use machines to pay the bills, write the letters, and do the accounts.

This mentality extends up the job hierarchy to supervisors and managers. Rather than being asked to inspire, lead, and supervise team problem solving, today's managers are expected to monitor by machine and administrate by remote control. Lab tests are fast replacing training as the key investment in new employees. Computers measure keystrokes a minute, calls an hour, and miles driven a day. These measurements become ends in themselves, overwhelming individual judgments about the quality of work produced.

The strategy of relying on smart machines to replace smart, committed people tends to become self-perpetuating. As people are forced to work "dumber," managers use reduced job content to demand pay freezes and reductions, doing away with health insurance and pensions or any other rewards for loyalty, hard work, and experience. Jobs designed to make people replaceable encourage high turnover and a growing marginal job structure, with people working under short-term contracts or leases, working part time, and working in "temporary" jobs for years.

Yet growing evidence indicates that when the electronic foreman comes in, quality goes down. And experts looking at the failure of U.S. corporations to change work design as they invest in electronic technology have found that the investment often *increases* costs without improving productivity. Jobs designed to demand only long hours and no mental effort tend to waste information technology as well as people.

Computers, it turns out, are only as good as the people who use them.[2] The more corporate strategists try to design smart machines to do the work alone, the less flexible the product and the fewer the people at any level of production who understand how to improve product or service quality. As a result, companies invest in high technology to replace people, only to find they must expand the number of people at the top to try to compensate for the reduced know-how of those below who are directly involved in producing or providing services.

Inflexible, unequal, and top-heavy job design actually reduces productivity. For example, a recent study of successful and unsuccessful companies found that 99 percent of corporations with poor performance had an excessive number of "managers"—personnel with no direct production roles. Poor performers made too much use of machines and paid supervisors far more than they paid primary wage and salary workers.[3]

On the other hand, the electronic age offers an opportunity to improve productivity through a new job design that asks people to reach higher rather than lower levels of skill and mental effort.

Real gains from investing in smart machines will only come when we redesign work to require "smart," committed people as well.

A recent telephone company experiment helps illustrate the possibilities. In 1982, AT&T and CWA worked out an experimental hotel billing information system (HOBIS) at a site in Tempe, Ariz. The office of 100 telephone operators was reorganized to accommodate autonomous work groups, each in charge of a full range of activities. Operators assumed the responsibility of supervisors and rotated through administrative duties. In addition, they changed the traditional work monitoring practices by eliminating individual work measurement; average work time was measured for the whole group instead.

Both AT&T and CWA viewed the experiment as a success. Productivity equaled or surpassed that of more traditional offices; customer complaints and employee grievances were lower. As a whole, although some funds were added for employee training, the project saved money by reducing management salary expenses. And while AT&T divestiture ultimately led to the closing of that office, similar experiments are currently under way in Ohio, Florida, and California.[4]

System-wide efforts by strategists in Scandinavia and Japan and in various European corporations to put creativity and mental effort back into the workplace along with investment in new technology have produced similar improvements. Increased worker decision making and control, and reduced inequality and hierarchy on the job have proven to be advantageous in an electronic age.

Resources for Change: Federal Spending and Tax Reform

In addition to regulation, other world leaders are using national tax and spending incentives to reward private businesses that redesign work and production to emphasize highly educated work forces and advanced standards of living. As these policies take hold, the United States risks falling into a distant second place in the world economy, relegated to producing only those lower quality, more limited products that fit routinized "sweatshop" jobs.

It's fashionable today to argue that the federal government cannot afford to consider the quality of life for family and communities. Despite public opinion surveys and evidence from some recent state ballot initiatives that American voters support renewed public activism, national political leaders cite the federal debt as the reason to postpone necessary policy changes.

Of course, the federal budget deficit is a problem. The massive $1.5 trillion additional debt accumulated in eight years has made the nation increasingly dependent on foreign lenders at the same time that it has soaked up funds that could otherwise be invested in education, health, science, and research and development. And current high deficit levels severely restrict our future ability to cope with recessions. Yet the goal of federal deficit policy must be to find solutions to the deficit that help rather than hurt the economy and family standards of living. And analysis of the causes of the deficit point to solutions that close the gap *and at the same time* increase our national investment in people to improve productivity and long-term growth.

The crucial beginning point in developing such solutions is to understand that the main cause of the deficit is not too much spending but too little revenue from rich and super rich families and corporations. This can be seen most clearly by comparing revenue and spending trends with total national income (GNP).

This comparison requires taking Social Security spending out of the picture. Social Security programs are largely financed by special payroll taxes that flow into Social Security trust funds. These funds are currently running a huge surplus, amounting to more than 1 percent of GNP, and in fact have been a primary source of money borrowed to pay for the spending deficit.

Excluding Social Security, then, federal program spending as a proportion of GNP is lower than it was in the 1960s, 1970s, or early 1980s. Nondefense spending since 1980 has fallen from 9.9 percent of GNP to under 6.2 percent. Only interest payments are up sharply.

Figure 8.1: Federal Spending as a Percent of GNP, Excluding Social Security

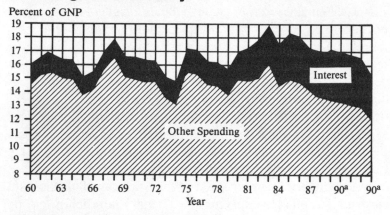

^aFigures from 1989 through 1993 are estimated.

Source: Citizens for Tax Justice, *Inequality and the Federal Budget Deficit* (Washington, DC: November 1988), p. 3.

At the same time, taxes, especially corporate income taxes have been cut dramatically. As a result of tax cuts initiated in 1981, total tax revenue by 1988 came to only 12.8 percent of GNP compared with an average of 15.5 percent in the sixties and an average of 13.8 percent in the seventies. Despite tax reform in 1986, the falloff in revenues is expected to continue into the 1990s (figure 8.2).

Only one income group has gained from the dramatic tax reductions: people earning more than $50,000—the richest 5 percent of all families. The Congressional Budget Office's comprehensive 1987 report found that the vast majority of American families are actually paying a higher share of their incomes in overall federal taxes today than they did 10 years ago. Yet Citizens for Tax Justice reports that "the effective federal tax rate on the wealthiest 1 percent of all people has dropped 10 percentage points since 1977. This amounts to an average tax cut for the super rich of $44,440 each—a 25 percent tax reduction since 1977." In other words, the same group of families that benefited from the redistribution of

Figure 8.2: Federal Taxes as a Percent of GNP, Excluding Social Security Payroll Taxes

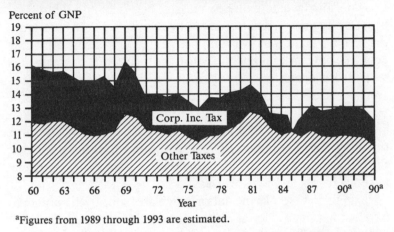

Percent of GNP

^aFigures from 1989 through 1993 are estimated.

Source: Citizens for Tax Justice, *Inequality and the Federal Budget Deficit*, p.3.

income *before* taxes received an *extra* tax rebate bonus from the federal government. As a result, the rich and super rich now pay a lower share of federal taxes, and their after-tax income has jumped an astonishing 74 percent since 1977, adjusted for inflation.[7]

Our richest families are rich by any standard. They earn an *average* of $452,000 each. Yet the tax "relief" given to them in the early 1980s amounts to a $45 billion tax loss to the federal government. The tax bonus for the wealthiest 5 million families—the top 20 percent—amounts to more than double the current annual budget deficit. And because of the deficit, the federal government must now borrow back the funds to pay for essential public services. The same families who benefit from the tax breaks tend to buy U.S. government bonds and Treasury notes. Additionally, interest payments on the national debt go overwhelming to the same upper-income families whose tax reductions helped to create the federal deficit in the first place.

Mergers and acquisitions further raid the U.S. Treasury. Current tax law allows corporations to write off buildings and equipment

at new, greatly inflated prices by subtracting the higher depreciation from taxable income. And merger strategists finance the change
in ownership by taking on new massive new debt and subtracting
interest payments from the remaining earnings. For the economy,
the result is a tax drain with no net gain in private investment in
people, plants, or equipment. If anything, jobs are lost as high debt
levels force layoffs.

The federal Treasury suffers a further tax drain from the way we
tax the business of multinational corporations. These corporations
are required to pay taxes on any income earned in the United States,
but current tax laws are inadequate to enforce this. In some cases,
the U.S. taxpayer even provides incentives for American companies
to move plants and jobs overseas.[8]

Tax reform that asks the nation's rich and super rich families to
pay their fair share to invest in the future could cut the federal deficit
in half. And reform of perverse tax incentives that allow corporations to profit through wealth redistribution could put federal tax
policy back on the side of higher standards of living and productivity. In other words, we *can* raise the revenues we need to tackle
the deficit and provide incentives to invest in America *without adding to tax burdens of middle- or lower-income families*. The following agenda for a progressive tax reform agenda illustrates how this
can come about:

Mergers and acquisitions. Limit interest deductions on debt used
to finance acquisitions and stock buyouts. Limit depreciation
writeoffs until they are realized.

Multinationals. Overhaul tax law to capture income earned in
the United States and stop capital movement abroad.

Depreciation reform. Bring tax treatment in line with the way
equipment and buildings actually wear out.

Alternative minimum corporate tax. Raise the minimum tax rate
that a profitable corporation must pay to 25 percent and remove
the ability of corporations to avoid paying the tax altogether. This
rate would still be less than that paid by most middle-class
American families and corporations abroad.

Alternative minimum tax on the wealthiest families. Currently, wealthy families can still escape all federal income taxes through legitimate tax writeoffs in which no real loss occurs. An alternative minimum tax of 25 percent would set a floor.

Higher tax rate for the super rich. Currently, the tax rate goes down when earnings top $240,000. Raising the rate on super rich families to 38 percent (compared with the current 28 percent) would bring in more than $30 billion a year.

The Task Before Us

To prosper and grow in the years ahead, we must reorder our priorities to invest in policies that build economic strength and ensure future economic growth. Through shifts in spending priorities and broad-based tax reform, the resources are available to us to guarantee a secure future. To harness these resources, we must reverse the course we have pursued over the last decade.

Change may be inevitable. The direction of change remains ours to choose. Current policies have opted for redistribution of wealth over investment in a growing standard of living for all American families. We must free up federal resources for child care, schools, workplace training, and venture capital for new innovative industries. We must demand that national, state, and local leaders redirect creative energy toward putting people first. The solutions we have presented are first steps toward changing course and improving the future for all American families.

Appendix
The U.S. Service Economy: A Portrait of the People, Jobs, and Industries

The People

The face of the labor force and the work people do have changed dramatically due to structural changes in the U.S. economy and the family. Thirty years ago, the typical worker was male, held a blue-collar job, worked in a large factory, and supported a family on a single wage. Most workers expected long-term employment with a single employer; they rarely changed careers.

Unions gave workers a collective voice in the workplace and paved the way toward shared post-war prosperity. Jobs provided the basic necessities of life for able-bodied people. Labor laws put few constraints on job policy, except to place a floor under wages (the minimum wage), require Social Security, and protect the right of employees to organize and bargain collectively. Social services, to the extent any existed, were targeted for senior citizens, children, and the disabled.

Today, there is almost a fifty-fifty chance that the typical worker is a woman and is part of a two-earner family, juggling the dual demands of work and family. Her job is likely to be in an office or in sales at a small worksite, although the parent corporation may be a multinational empire. She is also likely to change jobs and careers frequently in a scramble to keep pace with rapid technological change and international and domestic industry shifts.

Historically, service industries have relied heavily on the labor of women. Whereas women today make up 44 percent of the total work force, they hold 62 percent of all service industry jobs. Sex segregation by occupation is even more severe. In 7 of the 10 service occupations with the largest growth, women comprise 50 percent or more of the work force (figure A.1). Research studies estimate that roughly three out of five men and women would have to change jobs to end sex segregation.[1]

Figure A.1: Women in Service Occupations with the Fastest Job Growth, 1986-2000

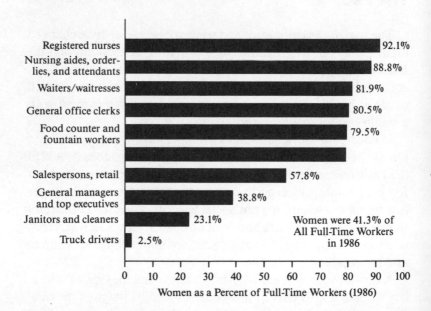

Women as a Percent of Full-Time Workers (1986)

Source: E.F. Mellor, "Weekly Earnings in 1986: A Look at More Than 200 Occupations," *Monthly Labor Review* (June 1987), table 1. G.T. Silvestri and J.M. Lukasiewicz, "A Look at Occupational Employment Trends to the Year 2000,"

Minority workers, particularly minority women, have typically found work more readily in service industries and jobs than in other industries and occupations. In health care, for example, black and hispanic workers make up 22 percent of the hospital work force; minority workers make up 32 percent of all building service workers. By comparison, blacks are 10.1 percent of total employment and Hispanics, 6.9 percent.[2]

Occupational and industry segregation has enabled pay and benefit inequities to persist despite the increased work force participation of women and minorities. A woman with a college degree still earns less than a male high school graduate.

And the typical worker is less likely to be a union member. Unfortunately, no other institution exists to represent employees collectively and acts as a counterbalance to employer power over job policy.

The Jobs

Department of Labor job forecasts for the economy point out why job opportunity no longer equates with prosperity. Although many new jobs created in our economy require high skill levels, 6 of the 10 fastest growing jobs are low paid. Many of the fast-growing jobs also fail to offer full-time work. As a result, weekly wages are at or below poverty levels.

—One in four janitors, the second fastest-growing occupation, earns the minimum wage. Half earn less than $4 an hour.
—Wages for nurse aides hover near the minimum. One out of three aides earns less than $4 an hour.

The media promote service economy jobs as offering high-tech and "information" age opportunity, implying a rosy future. Although technical and professional jobs have been growing rapidly in percentage terms, most job growth has been in entry- level, "old tech" positions.

Moreover, service industry employers tend to divide work into entry-level and higher skill, with few positions in between and little mobility. These hierarchies tend to trap people in narrow ranges with few opportunities for advancement. Managers have tended to adapt new technologies to follow the pattern, reinforcing the gap between wages and working conditions at the bottom and the top.

A recent study looked at the impact of different employment structures by comparing the income distributions of goods-producing and service-producing industries in 1984, using Census Data.[3] The study found that
—two out of five full-time service jobs fell below $15,000, compared with one in four manufacturing jobs;
—slightly more than one-third of service jobs paid between $15,000 and $30,000, compared with 45.9 percent of manufacturing jobs in the middle range; and yet
—7.5 percent of service jobs paid over $50,000, compared with only 5 percent of manufacturing jobs.

Service industry dominance and technological change have reduced the scale of worksites. Today, 55 percent of all workers work at a worksite with 100 or fewer employees, as compared with only 38 percent of all workers in 1976 (figure A.2). Only one in five workers today is employed at a large worksite—500 or more employees.

Often the worksite is in fact part of a large parent corporation. However, job opportunity may be confined to the site rather than to the employer.

This tendency toward smaller workplaces creates job instability and short internal career paths. Moreover, with the reduced scale of worksite, development of worksite-based training and benefit programs is more difficult. Without a city-wide base, employers often use the size of the workplace itself to argue against change.

Figure A.3 presents 1987 data on union membership by industry. Unions represent fewer than 10 percent of service industry workers in general and less than 5 percent of finance and insurance. Strong gains in the public sector have only partially offset losses in manufacturing due to closed plants.

Figure A.2: Size of Service Industry Worksites vs. Manufacturing Worksites

Percent of Jobs by Workplace Size

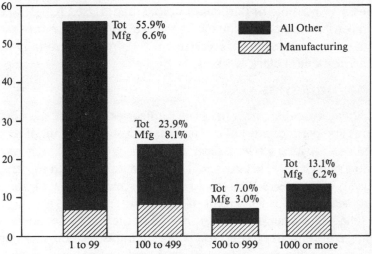

1985 Jobs Distribution by Site Size

Source: Bureau of the Census, County Business Patterns, 1985, table 18.

Figure A.3: Union Membership by Major Industry, 1987

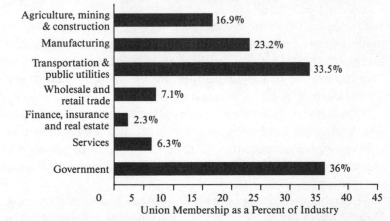

Source: Bureau of Labor Statistics. "Union Membership in 1987," News Release, USDL 88-27, January 22, 1988. Table 2.

Where present, unions matter. Overall, union workers earn 37 percent more than nonunion workers. And in each industry the pattern holds: services, plus 14 percent; retail, plus 50 percent; hospitals, plus 3-15 percent. In particular, unions have raised female and minority pay. Female union members earn 32.4 percent more than non-union females; black union members earn 43.1 percent more than non-union black workers.

The Industries

Today a complex array of service industries dominate the work force and produce most of our national output. Three out of four people work for a service industry employer, producing nearly two-thirds of the total U.S. Gross National Product (GNP). In contrast, service industries in 1950 employed 59 percent of the work force and accounted for 58 percent of GNP.[5]

The widespread publicity surrounding the service economy is often confusing due to the broad range of industries encompassed by varying definitions of services. In the most basic terms, services are defined as "intangible" products rather than as manufactured goods or farm products. In fact, services are perhaps most easily understood as everything that is *not* mining, construction, manufacturing, or agriculture.

Service industries are diverse. They range from airline service to public schools; from banking to health care (figure A.4). Retail sales and governmental activities are the largest individual service industries in terms of employment; they are followed by finance and insurance, health, and wholesale trade.

Service is also a job category that cuts across industries and professional status. And both manufacturing and service industries contain service occupations. In fact, 13.2 percent of all workers employed in a manufacturing industry work in a service or clerical occupation.[6]

The trend toward more people employed in services is not new. Despite recent publicity, jobs have been moving off the farm and out of factories since World War II. However, service employment

Figure A.4: Range of Industries in Service Sector

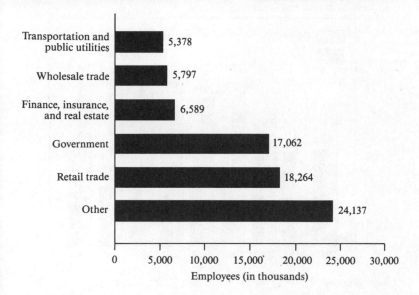

Source: BLS. *Employment and Earnings* (March 1988), table B-1.

growth has accelerated in recent years while growth in other sectors has declined. The number and proportion of people working in services, both public and private, moved steadily upward from 1947 to the mid-1970s (figure A.5), and the share of employment accounted for by services increased by 25 percent between 1957 and 1967. Since then, the share of service employment has increased by approximately one-third every 10 years.[7] BLS currently forecasts that service-producing industries will increase their share of total employment by an additional 5 percent by the year 2000.[8]

Retail trade and the broad category of "other services" provide the bulk of service industry employment, employing 17 percent and 22 percent, respectively, of all employed people.[9] Together these two categories employ far more than the combined total of the manufacturing, mining, construction, and agricultural industries.

Figure A.5: Growth of the Service Sector, 1947-87

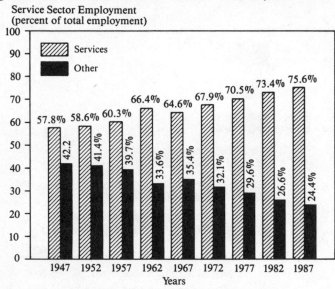

Service Sector Employment
(percent of total employment)

Source: *Economic Report of the President, 1988,* p. 297, table B-43.

Further, service industries have accounted for most of the dramatic U.S. job growth over the past 20 years and for virtually all net new job growth in the past 10 years:[10]

—Service industries (public and private) have added 48.5 million jobs since 1950; 27.9 million since 1970.

—Manufacturing jobs, in contrast, have stayed relatively constant since 1970 at 19 million jobs. Jobs are down by 2.01 million since their peak in 1979.

—Three service industries—retail trade, health and business services—accounted for more than 80 percent of the job growth in private sector service employment from 1960 to 1986 (9.7 million,5 million, and 4 million, respectively).

The Department of Labor and other forecasters expect these trends to continue into the 1990s, although at a slower pace. One recent study commissioned by the Labor Department projects employment in goods production to decline by nearly 2.5 million, with service employment predicted to grow by 23.9 million (32.9 percent) by the year 2000.[11]

Industrial and technological change also produced fundamental changes in the content of jobs. Today, the vast majority of workers are white-collar and service workers. Together these two occupational groups cover nearly 7 out of 10 people in the labor force (figure A.6).

Figure A.6: Percent of Civilian Employment Engaged in Service Occupations, 1987

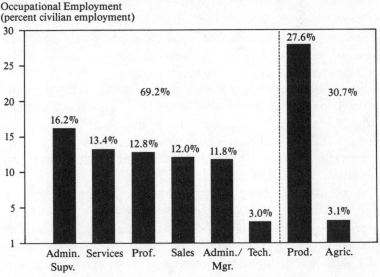

Occupational Employment
(percent civilian employment)

Source: BLS, *Employment and Earnings* (January 1988), table 22.

Despite publicity about the rapid rate of growth in many professional jobs, clerical and service jobs continue to lead in absolute rather than percentage job growth.[12] Between 1970 and 1986,

—clerical and office workers have led the service job growth, generating 7 million new jobs from 1970 to 1986, and today the number of clerical workers exceeds that of blue-collar machine operators and laborers;[13]

—jobs in service occupations have increased by 5 million;

—professional and technical jobs have increased by 6.1 million, including all jobs in both professional and technical classifications; and

—craft work and basic labor jobs have declined by 2.6 million.

A similar occupational shift has occurred *within* goods-producing industries. While automation has reduced the demand for production labor, managerial, administrative, and marketing functions are increasing white-collar employment in manufacturing industries.

Manufacturing industries require an increasingly complex set of services to survive and compete in a integrated world economy. Financial structures, communications, and transportation services have all grown and evolved to meet the needs of multinational markets and multinational production sites.

At the same time, the growth of service industries has depended in turn on the existence and growth of U.S. manufacturing. Manufacturing industries consume a large share of all business services. U.S.-based financial, transportation, and communication corporations have grown as U.S. multinational manufacturing corporations have expanded.

A quarter of the GNP originates in services supplied to goods-producing industries, and even more is linked through purchasing power of goods-producing employees and their families. Growth in the high value added, and frequently higher wage, service jobs depends upon maintenance of a strong manufacturing base. In turn, manufacturing growth depends on expansion of service industries to facilitate production.

A service economy does *not* mean that workers are working in food and other consumer service industries instead of in goods production. Only 40 percent of all private sector workers work in the direct personal service industries. And 12 percent of these work in health care or education. In contrast, 60 percent of service industry workers work to package, finance, insure, distribute, or sell manufactured products.

The other major service industry division, government services, covers a broad range of jobs and activities. Three out of four among the 16.7 million women and men employed by federal, state, and local government provide the basic services to schools and police, and on roads, bridges, railroads, and water, that are essential for an advanced industrial society (figure A.7).

Figure A.7: Services Provided by Public Employees, 1987

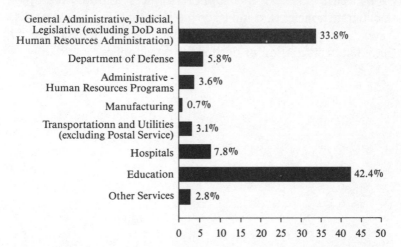

Sources: BLS, *Employment and Earnings* (January 1988), table 28. BLS, *Employment and Earnings* (March 1988), Table B-2.

In contrast, only 656,000 public employees provide social services for the unemployed, aged, disabled, or impoverished families with children. As with other industrial governments, public services support corporations as well as individuals.

Only a small proportion of total government jobs provide social or welfare services. In terms of nondefense expenditures, only Japan rivals the United States for last place in terms of social expenditure as a percent of gross domestic product.[16]

Summary

Our evolution to a service economy has been a gradual one, but one that, until the 1970s, ensured prosperity for American families. Our inability to accommodate rising standards of living over the last fifteen years is due not to economic change alone. Social job policy and labor law remain much the same as— if not diminished from—what they were 30 years ago. Jobs are still the primary—if not the only—source for earnings, training, health insurance, pensions, leave policies, and support services for the employed. Deliberate policies that fail to create jobs that pay decent wages, provide adequate benefits and some measure of economic security have led to stagnation or decline for our families.

Chapter 1:
Hardships for Working Families: A Corporate Choice

1. U.S. Bureau of the Census, "Money Income and Poverty Status in the United States: 1987," *Current Population Reports*, Series P. 60, No. 161, Washington, DC: USGPO, August 1988, Table 6.
2. See Appendix for a description of the U.S. work force, industry and job mix, and future projections.
3. Income is defined as before-tax income from all sources—wages as well as pensions, transfers, and investments.
4. Census data do not adjust family income figures for the changing size of the U.S. family. If family income is adjusted for the decline in family size since World War II, family income trend lines move up slightly for the period since 1970.
5. Sheldon Danziger and Peter Gottschalk, "Families with Children Have Fared Worse," *Challenge* (March/April 1986) and S. Danziger and P. Gottschalk, "Target Support at Children and Families," *New York Times*, March 22, 1987, Sec. 3, p. 2.
6. Bureau of the Census, "Money Income and Poverty Status of Families and Persons in the United States: 1986," *Current Population Reports*, ser. P-60, No. 157 Washington, D.C.: USGPO, July 1987), p. 31, Table 18.
7. Isabel Sawhill, "Poverty and the Underclass," *Challenge to Leadership: Economic and Social Issues for the Next Decade*, ed. Isabel Sawhill (Washington, D.C.: Urban Institute Press, 1988) p. 220.
8. Joseph Minarik, "Family Incomes," *Challenge to Leadership*, p. 53. Minarik uses an adjusted family size and an adjusted consumer price index to measure the trends in family income per quintile. Unadjusted income measures would show still greater disparities between the high- and low-income families.
9. Bureau of the Census, "Money Income and Poverty Status," Note 6, p. 13, Table 4.
10. Federal Reserve Bulletin, *Financial Characteristics of High Income Families* 72, no. 3 (March 1986): 168; see also U.S. Congress, Joint Economic Committee, *The Concentration of Wealth in the United States*, Washington, D.C.: U.S. Congress, July 1986, p. 23 and 30.
11. This figure is calculated by dividing the total number of employed people aged 16 to 65 by the population aged 16 to 65. People not working for wages (housewives, family farm labor) are not counted as "employed" in historic employment series. Historic comparisons are taken from the Census; current statistics are from the Bureau of Labor Statistics (BLS), *Employment and Earnings* (Washington, D.C.: USGPO, January 1988) Table A- 3, p. 15.
12. Joint Economic Committee, the U.S. Congress, *Working Mothers Are Preserving Family Living Standards,* Washington, DC: U.S. Congress, May 9, 1986, p. 2 and 3.

13. U.S. Department of Labor, BLS, 11 BLS Survey Reports on Work Patterns and Preferences of American Workers," *News Release*, August 7, 1986, p. 1.

14. David Obey, "Economic Policy and the American Economy: Lessons from the Past and Challenges for the Future" (Presentation of the U.S. Congress, Joint Economic Committee, January 16, 1986), p. 5.

15. Unpublished data, BLS, Office of Research and Evaluation. Although department labor analysts warn that the data has not yet been adjusted for potential differences in education and experience, the raw longitudinal data show a persistent pattern of lower earnings in the five-year comparison available thus far.

16. Minarik, "Family Incomes" Sawhill, p. 53.

17. Bureau of the Census, "Money Income and Poverty Status," Note 1, Table 12, p. 24.

18. Gregory Stricharchuk, "Retirement Prospects Grow Bleaker for Many as Job Scene Changes," *Wall Street Journal*, August 26, 1987.

19. See Appendix.

20. See Appendix.

21. SEIU surveys of Beverly nursing home workers in Michigan found families using Medicaid, the low-income health insurance program, for coverage. A 1988 study of giant Los Angeles county found that its 40,000 home health aides were similarly forced to welfare for a total taxpayer cost of $84 million per year, see SEIU "The Hidden Story of Taxpayer Subsidies for Low Wage Employers," *The Union*, April 1988, p. 4.

22. Manufacturing average hourly wages are down 1 percent from 1980 to 1987, adjusting for inflation. Service wages are up 6.7 percent over the same time period, inflation adjusted the gap between average hourly wages has closed from a 17 percent to an 11 percent difference, BLS *Employment and Earnings*, January 1988, Table C-1, p. 120 for hourly wages, and BLS, *Monthly Labor Review* October 1988, Table 32, p. 87, for inflation index.

23. Wassily Leontief "The Choice of Technology," *Scientific American* V 252 (6) June 1985, p. 39.

24. Bruce Nussbaum, "The Changing Role of the CEO," *Business Week*, October 23, 1987, pp. 14-15.

25. For a discussion of the U.S. failure to anticipate and prepare for competition, see Robert C. Reich, *The Next American Frontier* (New York: Times Books, 1983).

26. BLS News, *Union Membership* in 1987, Appendix 1, Table 2.

27. *Economic Report of the President, 1987* (Washington, D.C.: USGPO, January 1987) Table B-43, p. 294.

28. "The Outlook," *Wall Street Journal*, May 16, 1988, p. 1.

29. Kate Ballen, "Has the Debt Binge Gone Too Far?" *Fortune*, April 25, 1988, p. 89.

30. See Reich *The Next American Frontier*, for a further discussion of the tendency toward what Reich calls "paper entrepreneurship." (New York: Times Books, 1983)

31. National Academy of Sciences, *Technology and Employment: Innovation and Growth in the U.S. Economy* (Washington, D.C. National Academy Press, 1987)

32. See Stephen S. Cohen and John Zysman, *Manufacturing Matters: The Myth of the post-Industrial Economy* (New York: Basic Books, 1987); Reich, *The Next American Frontiers*; Michael J. Piore and Charles F. Sabel, *The Second Industrial Divide: Possibilities for Prosperity* (New York: Basic Books, 1984).

33. Piore and Sabel, *The Second Industrial Divide*, p. 264.

34. Henry Kelly, quoted in *Wall Street Journal*, May 31, 1988, p. 1.

35. Charles H. Ferguson, "From the People Who Brought You Voodoo Economics," *Harvard Business Review* 3 (May/June 1988) pp. 57 and 61.

36. Nussbaum, "The Changing Role of the CEO," pp. 6 and 28, *Business Week*, October 23, 1987.

37. Amanda Bennett, "Is Your Job Making You Sick?" *Wall Street Journal*, April 22, 1988, special Medicine and Health Section, p. 1.

38. Gary Burtless, "Inequality in America: Where Do We Stand?" *Brookings Review* (Summer 1987): 14, Table 1; and Sawhill, "Poverty and the Underclass," p. 217, Table 7.1. Both authors cite Timothy Smeeding, Barbara Doyle Torrey, and Martin Rein, "Patterns of Income and Poverty: The Economic Status of the Young and the Old in Eight Countries," studies of 1979 and 1981 data forthcoming in *The Vulnerable Aged and Children in the United States*, ed. John L. Palmer, Timothy Smedding, and Barbara Doyle Torrey (Washington, D.C.: Urban Institute Press, 1988).

39. Kjell-Olof Feldt, "Sweden's Third Way in Economic Policy," *Scandinavian Review* (Spring 1988) 76, no. 1, pp. 2 and 3.

40. Jan Egdal, remarks made at a seminar at the University of Massachusetts, May 26, 1988.

41. Bill Shapiro, "Cutting Costs with Cutting People," *Fortune* May 25, 1987, p. 2

42. Ferguson, "From the People Who Brought You Voodoo Economics," p. 55.

Chapter 2:
Declining Pay

1. U.S. Department of Commerce, Bureau of Census, *Money Income and Poverty Status in the United States*, Series P-60, No. 161, August 1988, Table 12, p. 24.

2. *Economic Report of the President*, 1988 (Washington, D.C. USGPO, February 1988) pp. 298-299, Tables B-44 and B-45. Data compares 1986 wages with those of 1972.

3. Richard Belous, The Conference Board Management Briefing, *Human Resources*, Vol. 3(5), May 1987, p. 4.

4. BNA, *Daily Labor Report*, March 25, 1988, p. 2.

5. SEIU Research Department, "Lump Sum Payments: Impact on the New Workforce," January 1988.

6. BLS, *Employment and Earnings*, establishment data series for 1979 and 1987.
7. Average manufacturing wage for 1987, as reported in BLS, *Employment and Earnings*, January 1988, Table B-1, p. 83.
8. Bennett Harrison, "Corporate Restructuring, National Economic Policy and the Worsening Distribution of Labor Income in the United States Since the 1970s," (Paper prepared for the Solutions for the New Workforce Conference, Washington, D.C. September 28, 1987.)
9. Barry Bluestone and Bennett Harrison, letter to the Joint Economic Committee, March 5, 1987; Aldrich Finegan and Frank Sloan, in *Moving Up and Down the Wage Ladder*, Final Report 1987 for the Department of Health and Human Services, HHS/ASPE July 14, 1986, 84/ASPE116A, also found that the proportion of low-wage jobs rose from 18 percent to 25 percent of jobs from 1970 to 1980.
10. E. Patrick McGuire of the Conference Board as quoted by Walter Guzzardi, "Big Can Still be Beautiful," *Fortune*, April 25, 1988, p. 64.
11. See special SEIU report, *Americans Deserve a Living Wage*, July 1987, for data and Tables.
12. California Office of Statewide Health Planning and Development, *Comparative Data for California Health Facilities*, Vol. 2, Long Term Care Facilities, FY 1984-85 and FY 1985-86, p. 114.
13. Bureau of the Census, *Money Income and Poverty Status*, pp. 15-17.
14. U.S. Department of Commerce, Bureau of the Census, *Male-Female Differences in Work Experience, Occupation and Earnings: 1984*, Series P-70, No. 10, August 1987, Table G, p. 5 and U.S. Department of Commerce, Bureau of the Census, *Money Income and Poverty Status in the United States: 1986*, Series P-60, N. 157, pp. 15-17.
15. For example, by 1985 more than 40 percent of the Canadian work force was organized, Morley Gunderson and Noah M. Meltz, "Canadian Unions Achieve Strong Gains in Membership," *Monthly Labor Review*, April 1986, p. 48, and Australian unions continued to gain members according to John Niland, "How Do Australians Unions Maintain Standing During Adverse Periods," *Monthly Labor Review*, June 1986, p. 37.
16. The proposed reform would have required an election within 30 to 75 days after a majority of employees signed a petition for a vote; an increase in the penalty for illegally firing an employee for union activities to 150 percent of lost wages minus other earned income; and penalties for failing to bargain once an election was won. Canadian law goes further. Representation rights become automatic without a vote once the majority of workers (over 50 percent by federal law) join the union. Provincial law further strengthens worker rights to collective action once workers are organized.
17. Hearings before the U.S. House Subcommittee on Labor Management Relations, April 1, 1982. Congress ultimately banned use of Medicare funds for anti-union consultants in September, 1982. The regulations were effective September 3, 1982.

18. BLS, "Union Membership in 1987," January 22, 1988.
19. Thomas Byrne Edsall, *The New Politics of Inequality* (New York: Norton, 1984) p. 142.
20. Uniforce Temporary Personnel, Inc. survey of 594 corporate managers as reported in the *Wall Street Journal*, April 28, 1987, p. 1, Col. 5.
21. Larry Schein, The Conference Board Management Briefing, *Human Resources*, Vol 3(6), June 1987, p. 1.
22. Emily Smith, Jody Brott, Alice Cuneo, Jo Ellen Davis, "Stress: The Test Americans Are Failing," *Business Week*, April 18, 1988, pp. 74-76.
23. Emily Smith, Jody Brott, Alice Cuneo, Jo Ellen Davis, "Stress: The Test Americans Are Failing," p. 74.
24. Starch INRA Hooper Survey of Workers in the United States, Europe, and Japan, as reported in the *Wall Street Journal*, June 28, 1988. p. 1.
25. For studies . . . Isaac Shapiro, *No Escape*, Center of Budget and Policy Priorities, June 1987; F. Gerard Adams, *Increasing the Minimum Wage: The Macroeconomic Impacts,* Economic Policy Institute Briefing Paper, July 1987.

Chapter 3:
The Contingent Work Force:
Part-Time, Temporary, and Contract Workers

1. David Kirkpatrick, "Smart New Ways to Use Temps," *Fortune*, February 15, 1988, p. 111.
2. The Conference Board, "A Contingent Work Force: The Wave of the Future?" *Management Briefing Paper,* (Sept., 87) Vol 3, No. 9, p. 1; Richard Belous, "The Job Machine Sputters," *Across the Board* (Jan. 1988) pp. 4-6.
3. Between 1979 and 1988, involuntary part-time work grew by 30 percent, compared with a 15 percent increase for voluntary part- time work. BLS. *Handbook of Labor Statistics*, Bulletin 2217 (June 1985) Tables 20 and 21, pp. 56-58; BLS, *Employment and Earnings* (May 1988) Tables A-35, p. 40.
4. BLS, "BLS Survey on Work Patterns and Preferences of American Workers," August 7, 1986. p. 1.
5. Eileen Applebaum, "Restructuring Work: Temporary, Part-Time, and At-Home Employment," in *Computer Chips and Paper Clips: Technology and Women's Employment*, ed. Heidi Hartmann, vol. 2 (Washington, D.C.: National Academy Press, 1987) pp. 284-285. For more information see Sar Levitan and Elizabeth Conway, "Part Time Employment: Living on Half-Rations," George Washington University Center for Social Policy Studies, February 3, 1988; and Garth Mangum, Donald Mayall, and Kristen Nelson, "The Temporary Help Industry: A Response to the Dual Internal Labor Market," *Industrial and Labor Relations Review* 38 (July 1985).
6. David Kirkpatrick, "Smart New Ways to Use Temps," p. 112.
7. David Kirkpatrick, "Smart New Ways to Use Temps," p. 110.
8. Michael J. McCarthy, "Managers Face Dilemma with Temps," *Wall Street Journal*, April 5, 1988, p. 39.

9. In 1983, part-timers earned an average of $4.50 an hour, compared with $7.80 for full-timers. See Applebaum, "Restructuring Work," pp. 284-285. The wage comparisons are based on 1983 data.

10. Congressional Research Service, "Health Insurance and the Uninsured: Background Data and Analysis" (Washington, D.C.: USGPO, May 1988)

11. BLS, "BLS Reports on its First Survey of Pay and Employee Benefits in the Temporary Help Industry," May 24, 1988.

12. Emily S. Andrews, *The Changing Profile of Pensions in America* (Washington, D.C.: Employee Benefit Research Institute, 1985) p. 49.

13. BLS, "BLS Reports on its First Survey of Pay and Employee Benefits in the Temporary Help Industry," p. 8.

14. Amanda Bennett, "As Big Firms Continue to Trim Their Staffs, Two-Tier Setup Emerges," *Wall Street Journal*, May 4, 1987, p. 20.

15. Connie R. Curran, summary of American Hospital Association (AHA) presentation to the International Conference on Nurse Recruitment and Retention in Long-Term Care, January 6-8, 1988.

16. Over the years, courts have come to define an independent contractor as someone who exercises significant control over the manner in which work is performed; has the opportunity to make a profit or to incur a loss based on managerial skill; invests in equipment and materials; maintains a temporary relationship with an employer; and renders a service that is not an integral part of the employer's business.

17. Kathleen Christensen, "A Hard Day's Work in the Electronic Cottage," *Across the Board* (April 1987), p. 20; Roderick MacKenzie, testimony presented before the House Committee on Government Operations, Subcommittee on Employment and Housing, February 26, 1986.

18. *Federal Procurement Data System Standard Report: October 1, 1986-September 30, 1987* (Washington, D.C.: Federal Procurement Data Center, January 25, 1988) pp. 2 and 3; David Seader, "Privatization and America's Cities," *Public Management*, 68 (December 1986) p. 7; Touche-Ross International, "Privatization in America: An Opinion Survey of City and County Governments on Their Use of Privatization and Infrastructure Needs" U.S. General Services Administration, Federal Procurement Data Center, (Washington, D.C. 1987) p. 2.

19. SEIU, Research Department.

20. SEIU, *Contracting Out: How to Fight Back and Win*, p. 42.

21. Bob Edgell, "Actual Cost to Contract Out Compared to Contractor and In-House Bids" (Unpublished report prepared by the American Federation of Government Employees, February 1987). For more information, contact AFGE, 80 F Street, NW, Washington, D.C. 20001.

22. 9to5, National Association of Working Women, *Working at the Margins: Part-Time and Temporary Workers in the United States* (Cleveland, Ohio: September 1986) p. 31.

23. Barbara J. Cooke, "Temporary Nursing Personnel in Ohio: An Exploratory Analysis" (Paper prepared for the Ohio Department of Public Health, State Health Planning and Development Agency, Office of Health Information and Research, May 1979); BNA, *The Changing Workplace: New Directions in Staffing and Scheduling* (Washington, D.C.: BNA, 1986) p. 12.
24. A 1987 study by the Hay Group, a human resource consulting firm, cited in David Kirkpatrick, "Smart New Ways to Use Temps," p. 112.
25. Michael J. McCarthy, "Managers Face Dilemma with Temps," p. 39.
26. Amanda Bennett, "Survivors on Corporate Staffs Yearn for the Security of Yore," *Wall Street Journal*, May 4, 1987, p. 20.
27. Michael Cooper, Strategic Management Associates, quoted in Amanda Bennett, "As Big Firms Continue to Trim Their Staffs, Two-Tier Setup Emerges," p. 20.
28. Quoted in David Kirkpatrick, "Smart New Ways to Use Temps," p. 116.

Chapter 4:
The Erosion of Employee Benefits

1. Office of Management and Budget, Special Analysis, Budget of the United States Government, fiscal year 1977, January 1976.
2. Estimates on the uninsured population come from the annual March supplements to the Current Population Surveys (CPS) prepared by the Congressional Research Service (CRS). CPS is a national representative survey of 155,000 people conducted by the Bureau of the Census. See CRS, *Health Insurance and the Uninsured: Background Data and Analysis*, p. 110.
3. Andrews, *The Changing Profile of Pensions in America*, p. 49. The Employee Benefit Research Institute (EBRI) also provided the 1985 estimates of pension coverage of the civilian work force.
4. Estimates are from HHS, Health Care Financing Administration, Office of the Actuary. See *Health Care Financing Review* 8 (Summer 1987) Table 12.
5. National Commission to Prevent Infant Mortality, *Death Before Life: The Tragedy of Infant Mortality*, (Washington, D.C.: August 1988) pp. 8-9.
6. Albert Sui et al., "Inappropriate Use of Hospitals in a Randomized Trial of Health Insurance Plans," *New England Journal of Medicine*, November 13, 1986, Vol. 315, No. 20, pp. 1261-1262.
7. Nationwide, hospitals' total unsponsored care (charity care and bad debt less any state and local government appropriations received by the hospitals) reached nearly $7 billion in 1986, more than double the 1982 rate. (AHA estimates). In addition, states spent more than $2.3 billion on medical relief programs, and cities and counties contributed $12 billion in noncapital support to public hospitals in 1984. Adding in other public subsidies—for example, tax-exempt bond financing and support to non-profit hospitals—raises the amount of public subsidies even higher.

8. This tax rate is the ratio of unsponsored care costs to the costs associated with private paying patients. See AHA, *Cost and Compassion: Recommendations for Avoiding a Crisis in Care for the Medically Indigent* (Chicago, Ill: AHA, 1986), pp. 6 and 52.

9. EBRI, "A Profile of the Nonelderly Population Without Health Insurance," Issue Brief 66, May 1987, p. 20, Table 12.

10. CRS, *Health Insurance and the Uninsured: Background Data and Analysis*, p. 100.

11. EBRI, "A Profile of the Nonelderly Population Without Health Insurance," p. 5.

12. EBRI, "A Profile of the Nonelderly Population Without Health Insurance," p. 17.

13. CRS, *Health Insurance and the Uninsured: Background Data and Analysis*, p. 97, and Hewitt Associates, *Benefits for Part-Time Employees* (Lincolnshire, Illinois: Hewitt Associates, 1985) p. 11.

14. BLS, "BLS Reports on its First Survey of Pay and Employee Benefits in the Temporary Help Industry."

15. Several features of health insurance plans determine out-of-pocket exposures: 1) enrollees often have to pay a share of the premium cost; 2) enrollees must also pay the full cost of any excluded services; 3) even for medical expenses included in the plan, enrollees are generally responsible for a "deductible"—an initial payment for covered services; 4) after the deductible is paid, enrollees may have to pay a percentage of costs incurred for covered services, usually 20 percent. Note that some plans have annual limits on these "coinsurance payments."

16. SEIU Research Department, "Access to Healthcare, A Survey of Service Workers," June 1987, pp. 1-6.

17. BLS, *Employee Benefits in Medium and Large Firms* (Washington, D.C.: USGPO June 1987) pp. 27-32.

18. Hay Huggins, *Benefits Report*, 1977 and 1987, as reported by the CRS, *Health Insurance and the Uninsured: Background Data and Analysis*, p. 51.

19. EBRI, "Public and Private Issues in Financing Health Care for Children," Issue Brief 79, June 1988, p. 1.

20. SEIU Research Department, "Access to Healthcare, A Survey of Service Workers," June 1987, pp. 1-6.

21. SEIU Research Department, "Access to Healthcare, A Survey of Service Workers," June 1987, p. 1.

22. Robert Wood Johnson Foundation, *Access to Healthcare in the United States: Results of a 1986 Survey*, No. 2 (Princeton: Robert Wood Johnson Foundation, 1987) pp. 1-10.

23. CRS Analysis of 1986 Health Interview Survey. See CRS, *Health Insurance and the Uninsured: Background Data and Analysis*, p. 137.

24. House Select Committee on Children, Youth, and Families, *Opportunities for Success: Cost-Effective Programs for Children, Update 1988*. Congress, Second Session 1988 (Washington: USGPO, 1988) pp. 1-72.

25. Data on the work force come from a special survey conducted by EBRI and HHS in May 1983 by the Bureau of the Census in selected years (1972, 1979, and 1983). Another survey is in progress for 1988. See Andrews, *The Changing Profile of Pensions in America*, Appendix, for further details on the survey.

26. Employers can terminate pension plans either to relieve business distress or to take assets from a healthy plan. In the latter case, they may recover plan assets in excess of the plan's termination liability (the accrued benefits earned by employees at that date). Since most pension plans base benefits on final earnings, workers can lose a considerable value of their pensions.

27. Bureau of the Census, *Current Population Reports*, Series P- 60, No. 155 (Washington, D.C.: USGPO, 1987).

28. Andrews, *The Changing Profile of Pensions in America*, p. 49.

29. Andrews, *The Changing Profile of Pensions in America*, p. 49.

30. Andrews, *The Changing Profile of Pensions in America*, p. 49.

31. BLS, *Employment and Earnings* (Washington, D.C.: USGPO) March 1987, p. 110.

32. 9to5, National Association of Working Women, *Social Insecurity: The Economic Marginalization of Older Workers* (Cleveland, Ohio: 9to5, National Association of Working Women, 1988).

33. Pension data came from Spenser Research Reports "Census Bureau Data on 1984 Pension Coverage, Retirement Income; 67 percent of Workers Covered," pp. 11-87.

34. Robert E. Hall, "The Importance of Lifetime Jobs in the U.S. Economy," *American Economic Review* 72 (September 1982) pp. 176-224.

35. This 1988 study, conducted by Hay/Higgins under contract to the Department of Labor, measures the benefit loss due to job changes as the difference between workers' actual benefits received under a succession of pension plans and the total benefits that would have accrued if the worker was covered under the last employer's pension plan over an entire career.

36. American Association of Retired Persons, testimony before the House Subcommittee on Ways and Means on Pension Portability, July 12, 1988. Using hypothetical cases of terminations, this study found that
    —a 30-year-old worker with 10 years of service at time of termination loses 92 percent of expected benefit at age 65 in a career earnings plan and 96 percent in a final average plan for which there is no successor plan;
    —a 55-year-old worker with 30 years of service at time of termination loses 46 percent of expected benefit at age 65 in a career average plan and 52 percent in a final average plan for which there is no successor plan; and
    —a worker with 30 years of service who loses a defined benefit plan of 1.25 percent multiplied by years of final average pay can lose 59 percent of their expected benefit with a defined contribution replacement that covers them for another 10 years.

37. Karen Williams, Health Insurance Association of America, testimony before the House Committee on Small Business, May 6, 1987, p. 7.

38. Small Business Administration, "Health Care Coverage and Costs in Small and Large Firms, "April 1987, p. III-15. This deduction is scheduled to expire on December 31, 1989.

39. BLS, *Employee Benefits in Small and Medium Size Firms*, 1986.

40. Andrews, *The Changing Profile of Pensions in America*, p. 157.

41. SEIU, Department of Public Policy, "The Hidden Story of Taxpayer Subsidies for Low-Wage Employers," April 1988, pp. 1-20.

Chapter 5:
Work and Family

1. U.S. Congress, Joint Economic Committee, "Working Mothers Are Preserving Family Living Standards," May 9, 1986.

2. Bureau of the Census, *Fertility of American Women: June, 1987* (Washington, D.C.: U.S. GPO, 1988.)

3. Sandra Hoffreth and Deborah Phillips, *The Journal of Marriage and Family*, quoted in Children's Defense Fund, *A Children's Defense Budget FY 1988* (Washington, D.C., 1987), p. 204.

4. Economic Policy Council of the United Nations Association of the United States of America, *Work and Family in the United States: A Policy Initiative* (New York: United Nations Association of the United States of America, 1985), p. 7.

5. Leslie W. Gladstone, Jennifer D. Williams, and Richard S. Belous, *Maternity and Parental Leave Policies: A Comparative Analysis*, CRS Report No. 85-148 (Washingtin, D.C.: U.S. GPO, 1985).

6. Sheila B. Kamerman, Alfred Kahn, and Paul Kingston, *Maternity Policies and Working Women* (New York: Columbia University Press, 1983).

7. Catalyst, "Report on a National Study of Parental Leaves," New York, 1986. For a survey of parental leave policies in small and medium-size firms, see James T. Bond, testimony before the House Committee on Education and Labor, Subcommittees on Labor-Management Relations and Labor Standards, "Medical and Family Leave Benefits Currently Available to Female Workers in the United States," March 12, 1987.

8. Catalyst, "Report on a National Study of Parental Leaves."

9. The Gallup Organization, "American Families, 1980: Report Submitted to the White House Conference on Families," Princeton, N.J., 1980.

10. Heidi I. Hartmann and Roberta M. Spalter-Roth, "Costs to Women and Their Families of Childbirth and Lack of Parental Leave," testimony before the Senate Committee on Labor and Human Resources, Subcommittee on Children, Families, Drugs, and Alcoholism, October 29, 1987.

11. William J. Gainer, "Parental Leave: Estimated Costs of HR 925, The Family and Medical Leave Act of 1987," testimony before the House Committee on Education and Labor, Subcommittee on Labor-Management Relations, November 1987; William J. Gainer, "GAO's Cost Estimate of the Costs of the Parental and Medical LEave Act, S249," testimony before the Senate Committee on Labor and Human Resources, Subcommittee on Children, Families, Drugs, and Alcoholism, October 29, 1987.

12. U.S. Chamber of Commerce Research Center, *Employee Benefits 1985* (Washington, D.C., 1986), iii.

13. Gerald W. McEntee, testimony before the Senate Committee on Labor and Human Resources, Subcommittee on Children, Family, Drugs, and Alcoholism, April 23, 1987; Karen Nussbaum, testimony before the House Committee on Small Business, August 4, 1987.

14. Louis Harris and Associates, *Children's Needs and Public Responsibilities: A Survey of American Attitudes about the Problems and Prospects of American Children*, Study No. 863009, 1986.

15. The exact number of "latchkey" children is in dispute. The Census Bureau estimate there were 2 million latchkey children in 1984 (Bureau of the Census, "After-School Care of School-Age Children," series P-23, no. 149 [Washington, D.C.: U.S. GPO, December 1985]). Other researchers estimate that the number is as high as 6 to 7 million, based on a national aggregate of local community surveys (Lynette Long and Thomas Long, *The Handbook for latchkey Children and Their Parents* [New York: Arbor House, 1983]).

16. Children's Defense Fund, *A Children's Defense Budget FY 1989* (Washington, D.C., 1988), p. 186.

17. Children's Defense Fund, *A Children's Defense Budget FY 1988*, p. 208.

18. Study by Saralee Howes, University of California in Los Angeles, cited in Children's Defense Fund, *A Children's Defense Budget FY 1989*, p. 182.

19. These figures are from The Conference Board. In a 1987 study, however, BLS found that employer-supported child care centers had become available in 25,000 of the nation's public and private sector workplaces having 10 or more employees. The reasons for the difference are threefold: (1) BLS uses establishments, not companies; (2) BLS counts include over 7,000 child care centers providing this service for their own employees; and (3) BLS includes schools and other public employers who have led the way on child care and other work and family issues.

20. This figure is based on surveys by the Work and Family Information Center of The Conference Board, a business research group. The BLS counts 25,000 business establishments with child care programs. According to Dana Friedman of The Conference Board, "the sample used by BLS was misleading because it included colleges and universities, public schools and day care centers, as well as non-profit employers, corporations and government agencies...Furthermore, BLS studied "establishments" with at least 10 employees. This means that IBM, with 200 work locations, is included in the sample 200 times." (Dana Friedman, unpublished Letter to the Editor, *New York Times*, January 21, 1988).

21. Fern Schumer Chapman, "Executive Guilt: Who's Taking Care of the Children," *Fortune*, February 16, 1987, pp. 30-37.
22. High/Scope Educational Research Foundation, *Changed Lives*, cited in Children's Defense Fund, A Children's Defense Budget FY 1989, p. 193.
23. Martin O'Connell and David Bloom, *Juggling Jobs and Babies: America's Child Care Challenge* (Washington, DC: Population Reference Bureau, 1987), p.8.
24. House Select Committee on Children, Youth, Families *Opportunities for Success*, cited in Children's Defense Fund, *Child Care: The Time is Now* (Washington, D.C., 1988), p. 7.
25. This number is based on the Department of Health and Human Services, "1982 National Long-Term Care Survey." The report on the University of Bridgeport survey can be found in Elliott D. Lee, "Firms Begin Support for Workers Who Look After Elderly Relatives," *Wall Street Journal*, July 6, 1987.
25. R. Stone, G.L. Cafferate, and J. Sangl, "Caregivers of the Frail Elderly: A National Profile" *Gerontologist*, v. 27, N. 5 (1987) pp. 616-626.

Chapter 6:
Employment and Training Policies

1. Total of 10.8 million workers lost their jobs because of plant closing or mass layoffs between January 1981 and January 1986: BLS, *Displaced Workers: 1981-85*, Bulletin 2289 (September 1987) p. 1.
2. Tables 12 and B-10. The majority of displaced manufacturing workers found new jobs in the service economy at an average wage loss of $57 per week. The new jobs were half as likely to pay health benefits.
3. Bryna Shore Fraser, "New Office and Business Technologies: The Structure of Education and (re)training Opportunities," in *Computer Chips and Paper Clips: Technology and Women's Employment*, ed. Heidi I. Hartmann (Washington, D.C.: National Academy Press, 1987) p. 369.
4. Sweden: 1985-86 Labour Market Board Annual Report; Singapore: Ira Magaziner, speech to Solutions for the New Workforce conference, September 28, 1987; United States: Office of Management and Budget, *Budget of the United States Government FY 1989* (Washington, D.C.: USGPO, 1988).
5. According to research conducted by Edward Dennison, "The Interruption of Productivity Growth in the United States," *The Economic Journal* 93 (1983), almost one-fifth of the growth in net national product per worker between 1948 and 1973 was a result of education. For a more recent review of the growth-accounting literature, see Rudolph Penner, "Economic Growth," in *Challenge to Leadership*, ed. Sawhill, pp. 67-100.
6. Shoshana Zuboff, *In the Age of the Smart Machine: The Future of Work and Power* (New York: Basic Books, 1988).

7. Howard N. Fullerton, Jr. "Labor Force Projections: 1986 to 2000," *Monthly Labor Review*, September 1987, p. 22

8. David Harman, *Illiteracy: A National Dilemma* (New York: Cambridge Books, 1986).

9. Cited in Robert B. Reich, "Education and the Next Economy" (Paper prepared for the National Education Association, 1988).

10. Carlton Braun, "Assessment of Immediate Training Needs of America's Workforce," testimony before the Joint Economic Committee, Senate Subcommittee on Investments, Jobs and Prices, April 12, 1988.

11. Art Shy, United Auto Workers, in a presentation to the Solutions for the New Workforce conference, September 28, 1987.

12. U.S. Congress, Annual Report of the Joint Economic Committee, April 20, 1988, pp. 46-47.

13. National Education Association, *A Nation At Risk Information Packet*, March 25, 1988.

14. The William T. Grant Foundation Commission on Work, Family and Citizenship, *The Forgotten Half: Non-College Youth in America: An Interim Report on the School-to-Work Transition*, January 1988, p. 26.

15. BLS, *Employment and Earnings* (May 1988), Table A-34.

16. Frank Levy, *Dollars and Dreams: The Changing American Income Distribution*, (New York: Basic Books, 1987).

17. The program evaluation literature finds that employment and training programs raise annual earned income between $500 and $1,500 a year. See, for example, Laurie Bassi and Orly A. Ashenfelter, "The Effect of Direct Job Creation and Training Programs on Low Skilled Workers," in *Fighting Poverty: What Works and What Doesn't*, ed. Sheldon Danzinger and Daniel Weinberg (Cambridge, MA: Harvard University Press, 1986) pp. 133-151.

18. Evelyn Ganzglass and Maria Heidkamp, "State Strategies to Train a Competitive Workforce: The Emerging Role of State-Funded Job Training Programs" (Washington, D.C.: Center for Policy Research, National Governors' Association) p. 1

19. For a summary of current programs, see U.S. Congress, General Accounting Office, *Plant Closings: Limited Advance Notice Assistance Provided Dislocated Workers* (Washington, D.C.: USGPO, July 1987).

20. Quoted in 9to5, National Association of Working Women, *Social Insecurity: The Economic Marginalization of Older Workers*, p. 52.

21. A recent review is provided in the Task Force Report to the Secretary of Labor on Plant Closings (The Lovell Report), 1987.

22. It is estimated that for the 3.5 million workers who lost their jobs because of plant closings in 1985, early notification would have resulted in $400 million saved unemployment insurance costs and enabled workers to earn $1.5 billion more than they actually did. Larry Mishel, "Advance Notice of Plant Closing: Benefits Outweigh the Costs," Economic Policy Institute, Briefing Paper, May 1988, pp. 1-13.

23. Paul Osterman, *Employment Futures; Reorganization, Dislocation and Employment Policies* (New York: Oxford University Press, 1988).
24. A 1984 survey conducted by *ITT Educational Services* magazine found that 44 percent of large corporations surveyed prefer to hire new employees rather than retrain current ones. Citation from Fraser, "New Office and Business Technologies," p. 344.
25. Osterman, *Employment Futures*, p. 53; and BNA, Personnel Policies Forum, No. 140, 1985, p. 37.
26. There is little data on private sector training programs. One estimate is that the private sector spent $210 billion dollars on training and retraining efforts in the mid-1980s—46 percent of the total $453 billion (public and private) spent on training programs. See Anthony Carnevale, "The Learning Enterprise," *Training and Development Journal*, January 1986, p. 18.
27. The new omnibus trade bill passed in 1988 folds Title III of JTPA and the Trade Adjustment Assistance Program into a new program for dislocated workers.
28. Richard W. Moore, Wellford W. Wilms, and Roger E. Bolus, "Training for Change: An Analysis of the Outcomes of California Employment Training Panel Program" (Santa Monica, CA: Training Research Corporation, January 19, 1988) and "Employment Training Panel: Report to the Legislature," 1987.
29. Quoted in Bill Saporito, "Cutting Costs Without Cutting People," *Fortune*, May 25, 1987, p. 29.
30. Paul E. Barton, A Better Fit Between Unemployment Insurance and Retraining (Washington, D.C.: National Institute of Work and Learning, 1986); U.S. Congress, Office of Technology Assessment (OTA), Plant Closing: Advance Notice and Rapid Response: Special Report (Washington, D.C.: USGPO, 1986).
31. Louis S. Richman, "Lessons from German Managers," *Fortune*, April 27, 1987.

Chapter 7:
Working Conditions: Health and Safety, Dignity and Autonomy on the Job

1. OTA, *The Electronic Supervisor: New Technology, New Tensions,* OTA-CIT-333 (Washington, D.C.: U.S. GPO, September 1987), p.9.
2. Zemphria Baskin, Air Transport Association, quoted in BNA, *VDT's in the Workplace: New Issues, New Answers,* 2d ed. (Washington, D.C.: BNA, 1987), p. 97.
3. Rebecca A. Grant, Christopher Higgins, and Richard H. Irving, "Computerized Performance Monitors: Are They Costing You Customers?" *Sloan Management Review* (Spring 1988) Vol. 29, p.41.
4. Case study prepared by 9to5, National Association of Working Women for OTA study, *The Electronic Supervisor.* For more information, contact 9to5, National Association of Working Women, 614 Superior Ave., N.W., Suite 852, Cleveland, Ohio 44113.

5. Case study prepared by the Communications Workers of America for OTA study, *The Electronic Supervisor.* For more information, contact the CWA Research Department, 1925 K Street N.W., Washington, DC 20006.

6. National Institute of Occupational Safety and Health (hereafter NIOSH), *Potential Health Hazards of VDT,* 1981.

7. 9to5, National Association of Working Women, *The 9to5 National Survey on Women and Stress* (Cleveland, Ohio: 1984). The conclusions are based on the responses of 40,171 women to a survey instrument placed in *Working Woman, Essence, Ms.,* and *Glamour* magazines. Data analysis was conducted by a team of academic experts and consultants.

8. Case study prepared by 9to5, National Association of Working Women for OTA, *The Electronic Supervisor.*

9. CWA and AT&T Communications, "The Emergence of Second Generation Quality of Work Life Models in AT&T Communications: A Pilot Study" (February 1986), as cited in OTA, *The Electronic Supervisor,* pp. 48-49.

10. Department of Health and Human Services, National Institute on Drug Abuse, "Employee Drug Screening" (September 1986), p. 3.

11. Victoria Churchville, "Applicants for D.C. Police Secretly Tested for Pregnancy," *Washington Post,* 5 November 1987. The Washington, D.C., police force suspended the pregnancy screening program until a written policy, including prenotification, could be developed.

12. BNA, *Alcohol and Drugs in the Workplace: Costs, Controls, and Controversies* (Washington, D.C.: BNA, 1986), p. 33.

13. OTA, *Scientific Validity of Polygraph Testing: A Research Review and Evaluation* (Washington, D.C.: U.S. GPO, 1983).

14. Ibid.

15. Richard M. Cyert and David C. Mowery, eds., *Technology and Employment: Innovation and Growth in the U.S. Economy* (Washington, D.C.: National Academy Press, 1987), p. 44.

16. Curt Suplee, "The Electronic Sweatshop," *The Washington Post,* 3 January 1988, p. B1.

17. Many other studies substantiate these findings. A 1986 study by the Center for Vision Care Policy at the State University of New York found increased eye strain, headaches, and back or neck porblems among VDT users. A 1987 study of clerical workers in Massachusetts found that employees who worked on VDTs all day had higher rates of vision problems and headaches than those who worked on VDTs for only part of the day. And a 1987 qualitative study conducted by SEIU and 9to5, National Association of Working Women, documents case histories of workers permanently disabled from their work on VDTs. See *VDT Syndrome: The Physical and Mental Trauma of Computer Work,* published by the Campaign for VDT Safety, 1987 (available from SEIU, 1313 L St., N.W., Washington, D.C. 20005, and from 9to5, National Association of Working Women, 614 Superior Ave., N.W., Suite 852, Cleveland, Ohio 44113).

18. Lawrence K. Altman, "Some Who Use VDT's Miscarried, Study Says," *New York Times*, 5 June 1988, p. 22.
19. BNA, *VDT's in the Workplace*, pp. 37-38.
20. "9to5 Campaign on VDT Risks: Analysis of VDT Operator Questionnaires," 9to5, National Association of Working Women, 614 Superior Ave., N.W., Suite 852, Cleveland, Ohio 44113.
21. John F. Brundage, Robert McN. Scott, Wayne M. Lednar, David W. Smith, and Richard N. Miller, "Building-Associated Risk of Febrile Acute Respiratory Diseases in Army Trainees," *Journal of American Medical Association* 259, no. 14 (8 April 1988): pp. 2108-2112.
22. Survey findings are available from SEIU, Department of Occupational Health and Safety. The Environmental Protection Agency (hereafter EPA) is conducting an extensive analysis of the data, which should be available in late 1988.
23. Anthony V. Nero, Jr., "Controlling Indoor Air Pollution," *Scientific American* (May 1988): p. 45.
24. EPA, Office of Pesticides and Toxic Substances, "Cost and Effectiveness of Abatement of Asbestos in Schools" (Unpublished internal report, 8 August 1984).
25. EPA, *EPA Study of Asbestos-Containing Materials in Public Buildings: A Report to Congress* (Washington, D.C., February 1988).
26. SEIU, "Largest Health Care Worker Union in U.S. Says AIDS/Hepatitis B Protections Aren't Working, Wants Program Broadened," Press Release, 19 Janaury 1988.
27. Michael J. McCarthy, "Stressed Employees Look for Relief in Workers' Compensation Claims," *Wall Street Journal*, 5 April 1988, p.   .
28. See NIOSH, "Psychological Disorders," *Morbidity and Mortality Weekly Report*, 3 October 1986, pp. 613-621.
29. Women's Occupational Health Resource Center, *The Stress of Women's Work*, 1983.
30. M.J. Colligan, M.J. Smith, J.J. Hurrell, Jr., "Occupational Incidence Rates of Mental Health Disorders" Journal of Human Stress, 1977; 3: p. 34-9.

Chapter 8:
Putting People First:
Investment and National Tax and Spending Priorities

1. For a description of how changes in ownership, including leveraged buyouts reap tax advantages see Louis Lowenstein, "Management Buyouts," *Columbia Law Review*, Vol. 85, pp. 730-784, 1985.
2. For recent studies see Paul A. Strassman, *Information Payoff: The Transformation of Work in the Electronic Age*, (Boston: The Free Press, 1985) and Shoshana Zuboff, *In the Age of the Smart Machine: The Future of Work and Power*, (New York: Basic Books, 1988).

3. Paul Strassman report on a study of the past 5-6 years as reported by Douglas S. Price, "Computer, productivity Link Disputed:, *Government Computer News*, 5 December 1986, p. .

4. U.S. Congress, Office of Technology Assessment, *The Electronic Supervisor: New Technology, New Tensions*, Washington, D.C.: U.S. Government Printing Office, September, 1987, pp. 47-48.

5. Unless otherwise noted all federal budget statistics are derived from Office of Management and Budget, *Budget of the United States Government, Fiscal Year 1989, Historical Tables (January 1988)*, and the Congressional Budget Office, *The Economic and Budget Outlook: An Update*, August 1988.

6. Citizens for Tax Justice, *Inequality & the Federal Budget Deficit*, Washington, D.C., November 1988, p. 5. CTJ draws its data from the Congressional Budget Office, *The Changing Distribution of Federal Taxes: 1975-1990.*, Washington, D.C.: U.S. Government Printing Office, October 1987.

7. From 1977 to 1984, the share of federal taxes paid by the richest 1 percent fell by 8 percent. As a result their after-tax income, adjusted for inflation jumped a 74 percent whereas pre-tax income was up just under 50 percent. Citizens for Tax Justice, Citizens for Tax Justice, *Inequality & the Federal Budget Deficit*, p.6.

8. See Citizens for Tax Justice, p. 11 for examples.

Appendix
The U.S. Service Economy:
A Portrait of the People, Jobs, and Industries

1. Andrea H. Beller, "Trends in Occupational Segregation by Sex and Race, 1960-1981," in *Sex Segregation in the Workplace*, ed. Barbara Reskin (Washington, D.C.: National Academy of Sciences, 1984).

2. U.S. Department of Labor, BLS, *Labor Force Statistics*, Derived from the Current Population Survey (Washington, D.C.: U.S. GPO, August 1988) Bulletin 2307, Table B-17, pp. 693-707.

3. Lynn E. Brown, "Taking in Each Other's Laundry—the Service Economy" *New England Economic Review*, July-August 1986, pp. 30-33, table 4, p. 25.

4. U.S. Department of Commerce, Bureau of the Census, *Statistical Abstract of the United States*, 1987, 107th edition, p. 409.

5. *Economic Report of the President, 1987*, (Washington, D.C.: U.S. GPOI, January 1987) tables B-11, B-40.

6. U.S. Department of Labor, BLS, *Employment and Earnings*, (Washington, D.C.: U.S. GPO August 1987).

7. U.S. Department of Labor, BLS, *Employment and Earnings,* (Washington, D.C.: U.S. GPO August 1987).

8. U.S. Department of Labor, BLS, "BLS Previews the Economy of the Year 2000," *News Release* 25 June 1987.

9. Unless otherwise noted, the source for industry employment data is the establishment employment data provided in BLS, *Employment and Earnings*. January and March of each year provide annual data for the previous year.

10. William B. Johnston, *Workforce 2000: Work & Workers for the 21st Century* (Indianapolis, Inc.: Hudson Institute, 1987), p. 58.

12. BLS, *Employment and Earnings*, January 1987; and *Labor Force Statistics*, vol. 1.

13. For a more detailed historical look at clerical employment trends back to 1940, see H. Allan Hunt and Timothy L. Hunt, "Recent Trends in Clerical Employment: The Impact of Technological Change," in *Computer Chips and Paper Clips*, vol. 2, Heidi Hartmann, Robert E. Kraut and Louise A. Tilly, eds. (Washington, D.C.: National Academy Press, 1986).

14. Stephen S. Cohen and John Zysman, *Manufacturing Matters*; The Myth of the Post-Industrial Economy (New York: Basic Books, 1987).

15. U.S. Department of Labor, BLS, *Employment and Earnings*, March 1987, table B-2.

16. Lucy Gorham, *No Longer Leading: A Scorecard on U.S. Economic Performance and the Role of the Public Sector Compared with Japan, West Germany and Sweden* (Economic Policy Institute, 1986).

INDEX